I0820666

Serious Fun

Serious Fun

The Landscapes of Claude Cormier

Marc Treib
Susan Herrington

ORO Editions
Novato, California

Published by ORO Editions
Publishers of Architecture, Art and Design
Gordon Goff: Publisher

www.oroeditions.com
info@oroeditions.com

Book Design: Studio Feed, Montréal
Managing Editor: Jake Anderson

1.9 8 7 6 5 4 3 2 1 First Edition

ISBN: 978-1-954081-01-7

Color Separations and Printing:
ORO Group Ltd.
Printed in China

We acknowledge the support of the Canada Council for the Arts and the Landscape Architecture Canada Foundation for their generous grants and their contribution to this book

For Stanley and Marco

Background

The comedian Mike Myers, best known for his movie role as Austin Powers, once remarked, "Canada is the essence of not being. Not English, not American, it is the mathematics of not being. And a subtle flavour—we're more like celery as a flavour."[1] Given this comparison of the country to a member of the daisy family (*Asteraceae*), and coupled with the fact that "sorry" is said to be the most frequently used word in the Canadian vocabulary, it is surprising, if not paradoxical, that the nation would engender one of the most brazen, and thoroughly unapologetic, landscape architects in North America.

During its first twenty-five years, Claude Cormier et Associés has produced a substantial body of work that is often daring in scope while earnest in execution. Although these landscape types have been diverse, the list includes virtually no private gardens. This professional evolution is quite unusual for landscape practice, where works typically move from small to large, from the arena of residential gardens to more sizable, often public, commissions. Instead, Claude Cormier's career began with a series of sprightly temporary installations—limited in size, yet large in ideas—that provided opportunities for his investigation of form, materials, color, as well as for their human perception and response. From these impermanent investigations, he garnered a substantial and more complete understanding of the complexities of permanent public and commercial landscapes. Under Cormier's leadership the firm has undertaken the design of parks and squares, renovated historical landscapes, and converted industrial sites, at times injecting a considerable amount of humor into both their method and the fruits of their labor. While the visual exuberance of many of Cormier's projects often eclipses their technical and ecological dimensions, in truth, his background in agronomy has informed and contributed significantly to the designs. Despite any degree of seeming frivolity, faced with the realities of climate, soil, and precipitation, his formal education in soil management and crop production has provided the science and the depth. These are further informed by social concerns, and those of form and materials. It is a practice unique in Canada, arguably in the world.

For those who live beyond its borders, Canada at times appears as a country with

1 Mark Kearney and Randy Ray, *The Big Book of Canadian Trivia*, Toronto: Dundurn, 2009, p. 132.

a lot of landscape but only limited representation in the field of landscape architecture. To some degree, this is understandable, given the vast size of its territory. Like the Nordic countries of Finland and Norway, Canada's population is small in proportion to its area. Added to this geographical dilemma, a population roughly the size of California's calls 3.8 million square miles home. Canadians have suffered an identity problem as well, particularly with the Americans. The Canadian novelist Margaret Atwood has called the border between the United States and Canada the longest one-way mirror in the world: through it, Canadians see Americans, while Americans look back only at themselves.

Perhaps due to this perceptual conundrum, Canada has provided only a handful of internationally known landscape architects and works of landscape architecture. Although Ron Williams's comprehensive historical survey of Canadian landscape architecture is filled with praiseworthy projects, many of these landscapes are not as familiar to people outside of Canada.[2] In fact, landscape architecture as a profession arrived much later in Canada than in the United States, and before the profession was established major commissions often went to American firms. For example, civic-minded parties in Montréal called upon Frederick Law Olmsted, Sr., to design the park landscape of the city's Mount Royal, perhaps the first Canadian landscape to achieve international repute. The American-born Frederick Gage Todd came to Canada in 1900 to work on the Mount Royal project for the Olmsted office, stayed, and became Canada's first nationally known landscape architect. Yet he remains not as well known internationally as the nascent modernist James Austin Floyd. The Canadian Society of Landscape Architects was established as late as 1934, and Canadian landscape architects of note have been slow to appear on the international stage. Indeed, many were educated abroad, as the University of Toronto offered the country's first Bachelor of Landscape Architecture degree only in 1965. It required an additional fifteen years for the University of British Columbia, located almost three thousand miles away in Vancouver, to instate a similar degree program.

Of the first major cohort of Canadian landscape architects, Cornelia Hahn Oberlander stands out. Oberlander emigrated from Germany in the 1930s and received a Bachelor of Landscape Architecture degree from Harvard University's Graduate School of Design in 1947. With her husband, architect and planner Peter Oberlander, she moved to Vancouver in 1953 and established an active practice that included a continued collaboration with the celebrated architect Arthur Erickson. Her landscapes have received widespread recognition for their noteworthy designs, both nationally and internationally. Deeply engaged with ecological processes and the social aspects of landscapes—as well as their aesthetics—she has authored landscapes in geographies that have extended from her home base in Vancouver to Germany, the United States, and the arctic territories of Canada's North. For decades she has remained Canada's most celebrated landscape architect.

While often quite different in vocabulary, Claude Cormier nonetheless shares several of Oberlander's concerns, including social responsibility and a deep regard for plants and their well-being. Both landscape architects lived on farms (Oberlander, during her teenage years) where they obtained firsthand experience with vegetation and animals. Having arrived on the landscape architecture scene some forty-odd years after Oberlander, however, Cormier brings a strikingly different cultural approach to Canadian landscape architecture. When Oberlander studied at Harvard, the school was dominated by the vision of modernism proffered by architect Walter Gropius and landscape architect Christopher Tunnard. Their ideas exploited the language of abstraction already witnessed in art and architecture, and through the postwar era landscape architects sought to realize modern works marked by the principles of civic responsibility, technical ingenuity, function, and economic thrift. In contrast, Cormier's Harvard experience was conditioned by postmodernism, in particular the thinking and designs of Martha Schwartz and Peter Walker, who jointly promoted a very different, more open—at times more formalist—brand of landscape architecture. They also helped revive the artistic dimensions of practice and emphasized the importance of history in landscape architecture that many modernists had denounced. Cormier's firsthand exposure to their ideas at the Graduate School of Design suggested to him that landscape architecture might also possess an aesthetic dimension that differed from the naturalistic or ecological models that had long dominated North American landscape architecture.

Soon after returning to Montréal in 1993, Cormier opened his own office and set about applying this revised concept of landscape architectural practice then taking root in the United States. His success was incremental, but almost immediate. That his practice has ranged from temporary art installations to the renovations of historic public spaces to the landscapes of residential towers testifies to the suppleness of his thinking and the breadth of his interests and abilities. That his office has received a plethora of awards from professional and civic associations confirms the respect which he has been accorded in his own country and abroad. That people use, and even love, many of his urban landscapes testifies to the humanistic dimensions of his practice and the pleasure afforded by many of these works. It should be noted, however, that Cormier is neither a sole practitioner nor a lone wolf, and in that sense his firm, Claude Cormier et Associés, is as much his willful creation as the designs that issue from it. This moderately sized atelier of about fifteen colleagues executes the design and research efforts, and guides their realization. Over the years, the office has become the proverbial well-oiled machine.

It can also be said that Cormier's particular brand of landscape architecture has provided a needed breath of fresh air to Canada's urban populace as well as to the landscape profession. The percentage of the country's urban residents has steadily risen; approximately 82 percent of the population lives in cities today, the majority of them in the country's three largest cities: Toronto, Montréal, and Vancouver. Of these, Toronto and Vancouver have enacted controversial urban planning and design practices that allow developers to increase the density and heights of new residential towers if compensated by capital investments for new or renewed public spaces, environmental restorations, or other "public amenity" projects. While this approach has supported the realization of numerous urban open spaces, it has also resulted in bland urban landscapes where the paramount objective is "not to offend." This is where Cormier's landscape designs have poked and prodded the status quo, by using form, color, and wit.

Indeed, his work has almost always been in the public eye, open to scrutiny and criticism, but also approbation and acceptance. Humor and delight, when suitable, frequently figure in his designs, which has led certain critics to pillory them as quixotic, frivolous, and void of substance or ecological awareness. Yet there can be little argument that projects such as Sugar Beach and the revitalization of Berczy Park in Toronto, and the

2 Ron Williams, *Landscape Architecture in Canada*, Montreal: McGill-Queen's University Press, 2014.

renovation of Dorchester square in Montréal are impressive in their innovation, formal skill, and social approval. Each in a different way exemplifies the breadth of the approaches taken by the office and the quality of the resulting designs.

In this, the first book exclusively dedicated to the landscapes of Claude Cormier and his team, we intend only to provide a broad overview of his ideas and practice, with discussions of selected projects and the thinking behind them. However, as historians and critics, we are interested not only in the story of how these works came to be but also in the issues they raise, both cultural and in terms of design. Among these are issues of kitsch and camp, gender, technical and biological expertise, and political, environmental, aesthetic, and humanistic aspects. In our respective essays we have attempted to introduce and discuss these issues within the context of individual projects and the narratives of their unfolding. These considerations and their bearing on the design idea—and its realization—are central to the story, whether the subject concerns flagpoles mounted on rue Sherbrooke in Montréal or casting life-size dogs in iron at a factory in Alabama. That is to say, the making of the place—which includes the selection and installation of its vegetation—is consequential to making landscapes, and as such has been central to landscapes by Cormier and his team.

Although there have been a number of publications about these projects in the professional and popular press, we have relied to large degree on what Claude Cormier has told audiences attending his lectures, and the ideas and observations he shared with us during our visits to his landscapes and his office and home in Montréal. A member of the team, Georges-Étienne Parent, accompanied us on several site visits and graciously supplied backup information when requested. We thank them both for their time, information, and insights. In the end, we truly hope that this introduction to the landscapes of Claude Cormier et Associés will demonstrate an approach virtually unique in the practice of landscape architecture, a practice rooted in social and ecological issues, but furthered through a manner of design appreciative of aesthetics, place, and even humor and delight.

Today much landscape architecture scholarship, as well as practice, has been herded to the safe ground of ecological viability and ecological planning as the basis of urbanism. While this approach was needed, these studies often yielded only elaborate diagrams of natural processes that analyze rather than design. In contrast, the landscapes of Claude Cormier remind us of the importance of realizing design ideas, the need for craft in execution, and the pleasure and beauty that may result. In this age of quantum uncertainty, with all its attendant threats and woes, we can use some comfort and a smile now and then and are thankful that Cormier's landscapes may trigger just those responses. Other projects, although perhaps lacking similar humor, nonetheless provide physical and mental comfort and please through their spaces, vegetation, relation to site and purpose, and all those other qualities that make a landscape worth our time to visit, pause, and enjoy.

A Note on the Book's Structure

The structure of this book departs from the more common manner of narrative, and thus may require some explanation. After visiting many of the landscapes and discussing them with Claude Cormier and others from his staff, we defined the issues that we felt marked the designs, as well as those properties that made them memorable and collectively constituted a practice that was

more or less unique. In our early discussions we identified themes such as biography and education, early employment by others, humor and wit in public places, kitsch, the use of plants, design process, beauty, sexual orientation, and social regard. We then divided the group of themes between us, each selecting those we wanted to pursue, understand, and attempt to explain.

As a result of this process, the two essays stand neither completely congruent nor completely independent. Some Cormier projects appear in only one essay; others are presented in both. This overlap of image and text, at times with some redundancy, is purposeful; in some places, the reader may even encounter differences in our opinions concerning the same landscape. The two essays can be read together or independently, following their order in the book or in reverse order. As a whole, the text is more a mosaic of ideas than a linear narrative, a structure we feel more appropriate to both our subject and our own thinking.

For all their efforts in helping us make this book the best it could possibly be, we sincerely thank Claude Cormier, Delphine Lesage, and Liette Locas at Claude Cormier et Associés, and Raphaël Daudelin at Studio Feed.

Marc Treib,
Berkeley, California

Susan Herrington,
Vancouver, British Columbia

November 2020

Claude Cormier et Associés
Team, July 2020:

(from left to right)
Carlos Portillo, Sophie Beaudoin, Yannick Roberge, Yi Zhou, Guillaume Paradis, Claude Cormier, Léonard Flot, Liette Locas, Delphine Lesage, Marc Hallé, Cloë Cousineau, Damien Dupuis, Amy René, Logan Littlefield, Alexander Cassini.
[Annie Éthier | photographe]

001
Sugar Beach.
Toronto, Ontario, 2010.
The beach in fog.
[John Ferri]

The Making of Serious Fun

Marc Treib

So, which of Claude Cormier's landscapes should we consider the most iconic, the most memorable, the most significant? Might it be—in order of decreasing subtlety—Sugar Beach in Toronto with its pink fiberglass umbrellas and carpet of sand [**001**], or the reinvigoration of Berczy Park, in particular, the ring of full-size hyperrealistic cast-iron dogs that spurt water into its central fountain? Or perhaps the vivid lipstick-pink tree trunks that thumb their collective noses at the prevailing grayness of Montréal's massive Palais des congrès? It's a tough choice, and our nomination will probably depend to large degree on what we consider appropriate for proper landscape architecture. To some, perhaps many, in the landscape architecture profession and among the general public, there is little room for humor when designing landscapes intended as environmentally responsible and socially supportive. Delight, they might assert, should be secured by means other than design features that border on kitsch. Trees and flowers and grass, and perhaps even a parkour for workouts, yes; these support use, please the senses, and provide welcome relief when spring finally arrives in the North and during the clement months that follow. But do we really need, much less accept, realistically rendered canines whose forms have simply been digitally enlarged from German toy miniatures and fitted with the necessary piping to spout water? The simple answer: yes; yes we do.

Formation

On a farm outside Princeville in rural Québec, Claude Cormier—born in 1960—spent his early years physically removed from urban life. Four buildings defined the center of the family farm: a large barn, a garage, a henhouse, and a ranch house that looked typical of the suburban variety [**002**]. Although enjoying the benefits of rural life, as he passed through childhood Cormier nonetheless felt that something was missing. To those years on the farm the landscape architect today credits both his love of the land *and* the belief that the land should be productive: after all, for his sixteenth birthday he received a chainsaw, a not-so-subtle hint that a tree can serve more than one purpose and need not stand forever. On the Cormier farm nature was controlled and directed toward production: it was a dairy farm with all the equipment and processes required to convert fodder into milk. From these rural years derive his respectful, but hardly romantic, regard for things natural and the greater landscape they comprise. Although Cormier retains fond memories of this pastoral childhood, he also confesses his childhood envy of the travelers who passed the farm on their way to or from their homes in

002
Cormier Family Farm. Princeville, Québec. Aerial view, 1970. [Famille Claude Cormier Archives]

the city, where he imagined the more interesting life could be found, experienced, and enjoyed. During these adolescent years he frequently felt trapped and dreamed of escaping rural life, to go somewhere, to discover something. He felt stuck in nature. This longing to be "going somewhere, discovering something" has provided a conceptual underpinning for his landscape architecture—to create landscapes rather than merely recreate nature.[1]

Cormier's father died when the future landscape architect was only seventeen, but not before leaving his son with the directive to pursue a degree in agronomy and apply the knowledge thus acquired to the management of the family farm. In response, Cormier first pursued an agronomy degree with a specialization in plant genetics at Université Laval in Québec City, but unsatisfied with the program, after one year he transferred to the University of Guelph in Ontario where he completed his undergraduate studies in 1982. He did not return to the farm on a full-time basis, however, but held onto his dream to "invent a new species of flower." While appreciating the knowledge gained through his studies in botany, horticulture, crop production, and soils—knowledge that would undergird all his subsequent work in landscape architecture—he felt that his direction was to be less that of the scientist and more that of the designer and artist. Consequently, he decided to pursue further studies in landscape architecture at the University of Toronto. Studying in Anglophone Ontario was hardly an easy task, hampered as he was by a quite limited ability to speak and write in English, the result of an upbringing in a completely Francophone and rural living environment. Nonetheless, he overcame this linguistic challenge and he succeeded at university. As a part of his landscape architecture master's thesis Cormier proposed removing many of the structures that then lined the banks of the Saint Lawrence as it passed through Montréal, to reunite the city with the river. A dispute with his thesis advisor over such ideas led to Cormier's completing the project with Blanche van Ginkel, a professor in the school's department of architecture rather than the landscape architecture department. This concern for bridging architecture and landscape, paired with an interest in the city and its natural and social geographies, characterizes his later practice.

After graduation Cormier first worked for about four years in the office of Diana Gerrard and Gunta Mackars in Toronto, and over time he began to understand the complexities of practicing landscape architecture. Perhaps here were sown the seeds for his belief that practice, in particular the process of accepting commissions, involves three Ps: *Project, People, Profit*—a motto he credits to his contact with the graphic designer Bruce Mau. At first this aphorism may appear hardline and Scrooge-like, but after some reflection one understands the logic that lurks behind it. *Project* refers to the nature of the work. Is it a commission that affords an opportunity for new thinking and inventive design? Is the budget sufficient? *People* concerns both the commissioning clients—Are they open to new ideas?—and the people who will occupy, use, and be affected by the new landscape. *Profit* speaks for itself. The fees must be adequate to support investigation and resolution within the office, and also adequate for the purchase of suitable materials and the employ of skilled labor in realizing the design. Perhaps the project need not generate enough profit to make a financial killing, but the funds must be adequate for making the job worth undertaking. As the Germans say, "Geschäft ist Geschäft," business is business; money keeps the office afloat and provides the opportunities for innovative work.

During his initial years working in the offices of others Cormier felt the need for

003
Martha Schwartz.
Center for Innovative Technology.
Herndon, Virginia, 1988.
[Marc Treib]

additional study to expand and enrich his thinking and design ability. While at Gerrard & Mackars, Cormier was part of the team then designing the parc Baile and the garden that accompanied the new Canadian Centre for Architecture (CCA) in Montréal, collaborating on their design with architect Peter Rose and artist Melvin Charney, who was its prime designer. Several years later, without sufficient savings to support graduate study, he approached Mme. Phyllis Lambert, the founder and benefactor of the CCA, with a proposition: If she would support a year's graduate study in landscape architecture at an institution with sufficient offerings in landscape history and theory, Cormier would consult on the maintenance of the CCA landscape in the future.[2] An agreement was struck. Now the question was, "Where to study?"

With friends, in 1993 Cormier took a road trip to New England. One rainy day, while staying in Marblehead, Massachusetts, the group decided to head to Boston and perhaps stop at Harvard University to have a look around. Their visit included Gund Hall, the home base of the Graduate School of Design; there, Cormier happened to encounter Martha Schwartz and immediately fell under her spell. He liked her personally, but perhaps more consequentially, he found her work refreshing, even inspirational. At that time Schwartz represented a radical wing of the landscape profession and was possibly its principal antagonist (for the best of causes, to be sure). Schwartz's formation and approach were rooted in art rather than usual landscape practice, and she tackled her commissions as artist and landscape architect in equal measure. In all, Schwartz had become a fly in the ointment of the landscape profession, not only as an outspoken critic of the status quo but also by the nature of her designs: landscapes that featured vernacular garden elements like mirrored gazing balls and concrete frogs gleaned from the local garden center (and she gilded the amphibians to increase their prominence) [**003**]. Her approach appeared fresh and conceptual, especially at a moment when design and art in landscape architecture had reached an ebb, their place taken by ecology and the analytical methods that reigned supreme. So Cormier decided on Harvard, but interestingly, not for its Master of Landscape Architecture degree—which would have required two to three years of study—but for a Master of Design Studies with a focus on landscape history and theory. Although he was frustrated by the omission

1 Claude Cormier, "Serious Fun," lecture, University of Toronto, Ontario, 31 May 2018, https://www.youtube.com/watch? v=fXIhtPhJgiE.

2 Cormier repaid this act of largesse by endowing a scholarship for landscape architecture study at the University of Toronto.

of studio courses in the program's curriculum, in the end nevertheless Cormier found the experience transformative.

Early coursework with certain professors provided little intellectual provocation for Cormier, but he cites his contact with faculty such as Mirka Beneš, Linda Pollak, Richard Forman, and John Stilgoe as important to his development.[3] Most important, his study year provided the time to think and reflect, to broaden the scope of his ideas about landscape architecture, and to formulate an approach to landscape architecture that in time he would make his own. During his studies he worked one day a week in the Cambridge office of Martha Schwartz, but after completing his degree he returned to Montréal. A first partnership formed in 1994 lasted only about a year, and in 1995 he opened his own office—Claude Cormier, architectes paysagistes—to some degree following a path blazed by Schwartz, although differing in its being informed and colored by his agricultural childhood, university studies in agronomy, and professional experience gained to that point.

On more than one occasion Cormier has quipped—with a smile, and perhaps even a laugh—that his two landscape architectural "parents" were Martha Schwartz (1950–) and Frederick Law Olmsted, Sr. (1822–1903) [004]. Schwartz's contribution has already been noted; Olmsted's requires some explanation. Given that Cormier's formation was rooted in his experience on the farm and in the countryside, he has always respected Olmsted's greater project to improve the lives of urban dwellers, while at the same time respecting the existing cityscape. What impressed Cormier most of all was Olmsted's broad vision, a vision that looked beyond the individual garden or park to the greater territory, to parks and parkways as structural units: what today we might term *green infrastructure*. Although Olmsted's design vocabulary and spatial ideas were rooted in the eighteenth-century English landscape garden and thus were somewhat dated even at the time of their adoption and implementation, Cormier found Olmsted's social vision modern in its quest to better urban life—an aspiration that Cormier shares [005]. The Cormier vocabulary, however, most often appears far closer to Schwartz's than to Olmsted's, and any version of naturalism in his landscapes has tended to occupy a rather small place in the practice, and even then, only where deemed appropriate. Like certain other landscape architects, Cormier holds that designed landscapes should differ in form from their natural state: designed landscapes are by definition human constructs—thus, artificial as in "artifice"—and therefore must

004
Genealogy: Frederick Law Olmsted + Martha Schwartz = Claude Cormier. [Chronicle/Alamy Stock Photo; © Martha Schwartz Partners; Industryous Photography]

005
Olmsted and Vaux. Central Park, New York, New York, 1858+. [Ajay Suresh, Wikimedia Commons]

consider additional issues such as those social, economic, and aesthetic. Perhaps Cormier might agree with Oscar Wilde who once quipped, "The more we study Art, the less we care for nature."[4] And like Schwartz, Cormier has always had one foot in art and the other in landscape architecture, although in his case landscape architecture, rather than art, instigates his considerations and usually prevails. Like Olmsted's early experience as a "scientific farmer," Cormier's upbringing with the routines of agriculture and maple sugaring, paired with his formal studies in agronomy, ground his designs with an understanding of natural systems and an appreciation of nature. This is not nature as an abstraction or romantic ideal, however, but nature as the set of universal natural processes necessary to enact and sustain landscape designs at either small or broad scales.

Rather than continuing this biographical and chronological narrative, at this point let us instead examine one recent project as a vehicle for addressing several of the questions and issues raised by the work of Claude Cormier et Associés. Among the foremost of these issues is populism, that is to say, the design vocabulary and imagery with which a number of his landscapes have taken form. A representative project is the 2014–2017 renewal and reinvigoration of Berczy Park in Toronto. Admittedly, in some ways this project represents an extreme—in other ways it is representative.

Going to the Dogs

Around the circular perimeter of the fountain at the center of the park, arranged on three stacked levels, dogs of multiple breeds and several sizes spurt water in streams carefully aimed toward the center of the basins [**006**]. Like the overall demeanor of the fountain, the tiered pools appear more than mildly Victorian, almost as if they had been recycled from some venerable font that had long occupied the place or had been imported to lend an air of history to this renovated landscape [**007**]. The bodies of these water-spewing dogs have been produced using two processes: the contemporary way, by enlarging toy canines using the wonders of three-dimensional digital scanning and computer fabrication, and the old-fashioned way, through the skillful hands

3 Just having the opportunity and time to read was greatly appreciated, and Cormier cites Elizabeth Meyer's "The Public Park as Avante-Garde (Landscape) Architecture: A Comparative Interpretation of Two Parisian Parks, Parc de la Villette (1983–1990) and Parc des Buttes-Chaumont (1864–1867)" (*Landscape Journal*, March 1991) as being particularly thought-provoking.

4 Oscar Wilde, "The Decay of Living," quoted in Susan Sontag, "Notes on 'Camp,'" 1964, reprinted in Susan Sontag, *Against Interpretation*, New York: Farrar, Straus and Giroux, 1966, p. 279.

006
Berczy Park.
Toronto, Ontario, 2017.
The central fountain.
[Michael Muraz]

BEARDMORE
BUILDING

007
Berczy Park, Dog Fountain.
Toronto, Ontario, 2017.
Concept panel.
[Claude Cormier
et Associés]

008
(opposite above)
Berczy Park, Dog Fountain.
Figurine sources.
[Claude Cormier
et Associés]

009
(opposite below)
Berczy Park, Dog Fountain.
Composition of canines.
[Claude Cormier
et Associés]

010
Berczy Park, Dog Fountain.
Toronto, Ontario, 2017.
Cast iron dog, painted.
[Peter McCann
Architectural Models Inc.]

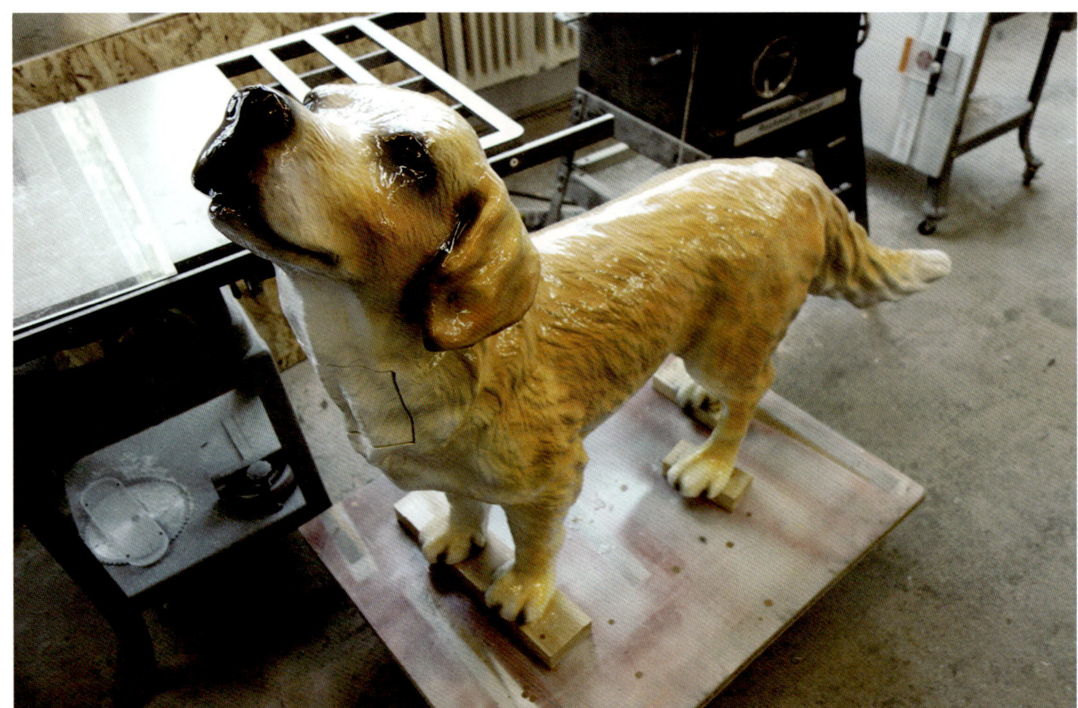

of the sculptor/artisan [008] [009]. The dogs, cast in iron at true size, have been painted in a realistic manner. Their surfaces are not matte; they are shiny and lustrous, at least they were at the moment of their installation [010]. The coloring, although faithful to the tints of the actual fur, is marked by a noticeable contrast in hue and tone, replicating in literal form the painting of the toy animals rather than the living canines that are their subjects.

Gaining the approval of the city's various review boards at any stage of the design process was not an easy matter. At first the landscape architects were faced with a wholesale rejection of the fountain's dogs and overall design, the argument being that, one, their "frivolous" character was somehow well below the acceptable level of design excellence for a Toronto public space, and, two, that canines are unsuitable for use as artistic subjects. Against this charge, Team Cormier prepared a visual presentation with images taken from the books *Best in Show: The Dog in Art from the Renaissance to Today*, by Edgar Peters Bowron et al. and Tamsin Pickeral's *The Dog: 5000 Years of the Dog in Art*.[5] Using some hundred illustrations taken from the books, Cormier educated the staff of diverse city departments by demonstrating that the genus *Canis lupus familiaris* had, in fact, been deemed a worthy subject for depiction by artists over many centuries. Just to top it off, they added a political dimension to their argument by including an 1809 portrait by William Berczy of the Woolsey family pictured with a favorite dog, and an endearing photo of Queen Elizabeth II, still titular sovereign of Canada, with her three corgis [011]. The battle was won; approval was secured and the project proceeded.[6]

Despite this success, certain parties involved with the design review process were nonetheless troubled by the feigned realism of the modeling and glossy surfaces of the canine sculptures; they suggested that monochromatic dogs with matte finishes would be more appropriate both for an artwork, and more specifically, as an artistic expression suitable for a contemporary park. To soothe their objections, Cormier prepared a second presentation, this one arguing that a significant number of contemporary artworks were marked by glossy surfaces. Once again, he was successful: minds were changed; once again, approval was secured. Without

011
William Berczy.
The Woolsey Family.
[National Gallery of Canada. Gift of Major Edgar C. Woolsey, Ottawa, 1952. Photo: NGC]

5 Edgar Peters Bowron, Carolyn Rose Rebbert, Robert Rosenblum, and William Secord, *Best in Show: The Dog in Art from the Renaissance to Today*, New Haven: Yale University Press, 2006; Tamsin Pickeral, *The Dog: 5000 Years of The Dog in Art*, New York: Merrell, 2008.

6 The painting, *The Woolsey Family*, is in the collection of the National Gallery of Canada.

question a certain festive aspect is gained by realistic coloration and paired with the circular arrangement of the dogs around the stacked bowls of the fountain, the impression might even trigger memories of carousel animals, which are often painted with colors and marked by contrasts that border on the lurid.[7] In the end, however, all aspects of the project regarding form, reference, and rendering were accepted; construction proceeded apace, and the park opened in 2017 to overwhelmingly popular approbation.

Although the park landscape provides amenity, comfort, and delight far beyond that offered by the dog pack alone, the fountain is without question the park's most memorable attribute. The fountain is literally attractive, charming both living canines and the bipeds who care for them and with whom they live. It is without question a pleasant feature: its constituent elements are magnetic, appealing to people of all ages who are drawn to the dogs and their waters as if by some invisible yet magnetic force. As they pass by, or stop and gaze upon the tiers of canines, virtually everyone smiles; some even laugh out loud. Of all the visitor groups, however, it is the children who seem to experience the greatest enjoyment, as in their eyes the edge between reality and its representation appears soft and indistinct. How can a child not enjoy encountering a Saint Bernard who spews water rather than drools, and kindly lets you ride on his (or her?) back without even the most minor flinch [**012**]? Perhaps to the child the dogs *are* real, real in a way removed from breathing animals perhaps, but real nonetheless.

It would be easy to dismiss the fountain as an exercise that at best qualifies as pop culture, and less kindly, as an exercise in camp or kitsch. While some might admit that given its friendly sensibility the fountain may qualify as some sort of "pop art," they might not accept that it would qualify as art at its highest sphere. Others might decry the realism of the form and coloration of the dogs as insufficiently abstract to warrant their qualification as art. Cormier himself makes no claim that either the fountain or its dogs qualify as art. And one must keep in mind that the fountain is but one feature in the design of a small landscape configured to support pleasurable life in the city. But what about this issue of popular appeal? Can we dismiss so readily the notion of enchantment in landscape design—and in the public realm? In the sixteenth century the English diplomat and aesthete Henry Wotton claimed that "well-building [i.e., worthy architecture] hath commodity, firmness, and delight." And delight. Is it, then, just a question of the relative ranking of these three factors? Which comes first? Commodity (volume), firmness (durability), or joy? Though by far its principal attraction, in truth the fountain is but one element of a handsomely reinvigorated green space and plaza in downtown Toronto. Let's now review the story of the project and the sources of its forms, and postpone a final judgment until after the complete story is told. Doing so will also lead to a more complete discussion of the landscape architecture of Claude Cormier and his team.

In some ways the parcel of land that is today Berczy Park was just a leftover triangle bordered by Wellington, Front, and Scott Streets measuring about one and a half acres in total surface area. William Berczy, for whom the park is named, was a German-born architect, painter, and surveyor who arrived in Canada in the 1790s after a short stay in the United States; he and John Graves Simcoe are credited with the cofounding of Toronto. The park occupies land in Toronto's downtown not far from Union Station and the VIA railroad, with the Sony Centre for the Performing Arts—whose plaza, as it happens,

7 This observation comes from my friend, photographer Nina Zurier.

012
Berczy Park.
Toronto, Ontario, 2017.
Riding the St. Bernard.
[Industryous Photography]

013
Berczy Park.
Toronto, Ontario, 2017.
Aerial view shortly
after completion.
[Industryous Photography]

BEARDMORE BUILDING
WINNERS

014
Berczy Park.
Toronto, Ontario, 2017.
Grassed mounds as buffer.
[Marc Treib]

015
Berczy Park.
Paving pattern with
historical precedent.
[Industryous Photography]

was recently reworked by the Cormier office—quite nearby on the opposite side of Front Street. The history of Berczy Park is, in fact, not a long one; its form immediately before renovation was a product of the 1980s.

That particular iteration of the park followed a model typical for its time, with a selection of spruces and pines used to create a sense of enclosure and to offer some interest to what was essentially a landscape of flat lawn and paving. A fountain with a round basin stood in more or less the same location as it does today, although dogs did not feature in its design. Well used and loved by locals and those passing through on their way to other downtown destinations, over the decades the park had nevertheless fallen into disrepair—despite the plethora of new apartment construction in the immediate vicinity. The regeneration of what is today the Sony Centre suggested it was also time to reinvigorate the park across the street. Claude Cormier et Associés received the commission for its redesign following the city's issuing of a Request for Qualifications from those firms interested in pursuing the assignment. Although open to other innovative ideas, in response to the demands of the local citizens group, the brief required that the amount of green space—lawn and vegetation—must equal or exceed the measure of these areas within the existing park.

The new design obviously centers on the new fountain, whose imagery and humor to some degree cast into shadow the sensible and sensitive reworking of the greater park landscape. The circulation planning of the new design respects the existing trajectories of those who passed through the park in prior years, that is, pedestrian movement through this quarter of the city. The plans for the green zones that resulted from this accommodation of circulation are hardly remarkable, or even noticeable [**013**]. This partial invisibility stems to some degree from the subtlety of the renewed landscape design and the nature of certain specific changes that are elusive at first glance. For example, in the former park the panels of grass between the walkways were flat; the Cormier design vivified them as volumes, shaping them into hillocks on which people can sit or lie and look out over the benches that line the paths [**014**]. Of the existing trees, eighty were found to be decayed and beyond saving; in fact, only ten trees were retained. New plantings of tulip poplar, elm, London plane tree, oak, and magnolia provide a physical and psychological boundary along Wellington Street and soften the transition in scale to the tower buildings that surround the site on two sides. There's also a splash of a mature pagoda tree and gingko trees on the park's north flank, and to the east a playful painted trompe l'œil mural by artist Derek Michael Besant enlivens the rear façade of the 1892 Gooderham Flatiron Building—visible to the left of figure. Also to the east, the terrain rises as a dog run and poop zone enclosed by a low fence. However functional, this area feels a bit alien to the remainder of the design, a land apart. Along Front Street, whose edge serves as the site's principal promenade, new gray and red granite paving has been patterned as a field of hollow squares that add a vibrant note and certain sparkle to the ground plane [**015**]. While first challenged as being foreign to the site by certain of the powers that be, the design in fact derives from the paving pattern in the old city hall located some few blocks away and, further afield, from certain plazas in Venice, or possibly even from the *cour d'honneur* before the château at Versailles (all these potential sources have been cited in conversations with the landscape architect). By extending the paving of the small triangular plaza across the existing sidewalk as far as the curb, the narrow walkway has been rendered an integral element of the park.

WINNERS

016
(opposite)
Berczy Park, Dog Fountain.
Toronto, Ontario, 2017.
Three tiers topped with
the Golden Bone.
[Industryous Photography]

017
Berczy Park, Dog Fountain.
Fountain rim in the form
of a dog collar.
[Industryous Photography]

018
Berczy Park, Dog Fountain.
The Golden Bone.
[Industryous Photography]

019
Berczy Park, Dog Fountain.
The cat.
[Industryous Photography]

020
Berczy Park.
Toronto, Ontario, 2017.
At twilight.
[Industryous Photography]

OK, so now we understand the functional and political aspects of the design, but why the dogs? For one, since its origin in the 1980s the park has been a destination for our four-legged friends and their owners [016]. While it feels a bit hard to believe, Cormier claims that some 1,500 dogs visit the park each day for one reason or another, or so it is estimated. However, from various websites we learn that there are 8.2 million dogs resident in Canada's cities, countryside, and wilderness, and that 37 percent of the Canadian population enjoys their companionship on a daily basis.[8] Although this number may appear impossibly high, and despite the precise number of canines that "give" and take in the park each day, their presence is significant. It was Cormier himself who conceived the fountain as a canine habitat; well, at least as an aquatic habitat for canines realized in cast iron. The fountain is arranged in three levels, each occupied by dogs of different sizes. On the ground, six large dogs offer up the longest arcs of water, among them a Saint Bernard, schnauzer, golden retriever, and Bernese mountain dog. These stand outside the basin and share spaces with humans and dogs that breathe. At their paws, a shallow circumferential trough offers water for the visiting pack that comes to drink. As a group, the dogs provide the lure and the transition between the outside and interior of the fountain, whose inhabitants include a male and female pug. On the second level, six smaller dogs such as a Jack Russell terrier and a beagle add to the splash. The belt circling this basin is configured as a studded dog collar at colossal scale [017]. Next up is a ring of smaller animals that include boxer and Dalmatian puppies, and crowning the composition is a golden bone, the Holy Grail pursued by all the dogs in and around the three basins [018]. In all, the fountain composition constitutes a canine world seeking heaven, graced by representatives of a variety of sizes and multiple breeds. The inclusion of two cats in the park's menagerie thwarts a complete canine monopoly: one cat is poised atop the mirrored utility box at the western entrance to the park; the second sits on the rim of the lowest basin with eyes fixed directly on the two yellow Canadian warblers that perch on a nearby light standard [019]. Will the cats cause havoc amid the placid world of dogs and water? Or will they manage to coexist peacefully, the dogs keeping to their assigned role as the sources of water for cooling and joy, the cats as static lookers-on? It's almost impossible not to smile at the tiny perfection of fountain and the landscape, both in concept and execution, and to enjoy the park for its amenity as well as its humor [020].

Cultures "High" and "Low"

Admittedly, no clear division distinguishes "high" from "low" culture, and mutual influences and exchanges between the categories have existed for many centuries. That is, only if we accept that a distinction exists between the two "cultural levels" at all. In the introduction to their book *High and Low: Modern Art and Popular Culture*, Kirk Varnedoe and Adam Gopnik underscore the problems involved with distinguishing these two classes when applied to art: "The theoretical literature on the division between high and low culture in modern life could appear to leave room for countless hybrid permutations among a set of terms such as elitist, populist, nostalgist, conservative, radical, optimist, and skeptic."[9] All these adjectives could apply simultaneously to the Berczy Park project, except skeptic[al], which the design is patently not. But to the list one might also add "ironic," as the line between irony and humor is often a very fine one. Irony, however, usually demands a ready and known referent whose familiarity unfortunately often diminishes with time. Dogs, on the other hand, are eternal. So rather than irony, perhaps "sly" or "with a knowing grin" are more apposite terms for the character of the new Berczy fountain.

Despite any arguments to the contrary, realistic recreations of domestic companion animals like these may easily be derided as kitsch or camp. Issues concerning figuration and overt references flow through many of Cormier's landscapes, troubling design review boards as well as some segments of the population. As such, the issue warrants some discussion. In his classic 1939 essay "Avant-Garde and Kitsch," the modernist art historian Clement Greenberg, operating at the elite cultural level of the art world, believed that kitsch used for "raw material the debased and academicized simulacra of genuine culture," and thus cultivated "insensibility."[10] A term German in origin, *kitsch* has come to be understood as referring to things corny, sentimental, and overly populist—things like gaudy images of Aztec warriors or clowns painted on black velvet, Schwartzwald cuckoo clocks, ashtrays made of tropical seashells and sand dollars, and salt and pepper shakers in the form of cacti or Plymouth Rock. These items may be attractive to some people while ridiculed by others, with the verdict often determined by class and education. To many in the art world, kitsch is simply those depictions or forms that have been denuded of their significance; forms which once conveyed ideas—and perhaps even represented invention, but forms that have now become hackneyed; forms that sell simply through their familiarity and perhaps manufactured in large numbers—in terms of North America, objects often produced overseas in developing countries at low cost. The mechanical reproduction of these objects in large numbers has injected kitsch into our society where it has been absorbed as an integral part of our material culture. Kitsch, then, represents a conflating of life and its representation, while according to Greenberg, for consideration as art, a distinction must exist between the subject and the artwork. Painting, then, is not about accurately depicting life as it is; instead, art should embody an act of true creation. Greenberg also asserts that at its root, a painting comprises intentional marks made on a canvas or some other ground.[11] Seen in this light, the realistically rendered dogs of Berczy Park are kitsch because their making sought to blur the boundary between life and art rather than to render that boundary more apparent.

While featuring the same canines and their same disposition, Cormier could have, for example, left the dogs unpainted, thereby achieving some degree of abstraction, as we find, for example, in the work of Jeff Koons. To create one series of his sculptures, Koons cast a selection of inflatable toys or balloon animals in polished stainless steel left silver, or tinted with metallic tones [**021**]. This shift from realistic to abstract, from a material elastic and short-lived to one rigid and durable, and from polychrome to monochrome, distinguished the artwork from the plaything—this despite their identical forms. We are familiar with the great lions of natural stone protecting Nelson's Column in London's Trafalgar Square, or those beasts

8 https://www.cahi-icsa.ca/press-releases/latest-canadian-pet-population-figures-released and https://www.petbacker.com/blog/facts/facts-about-pet-ownership-in-canada. This compares with 40 percent in Australia and 39 percent in the United States. Isaac Middle, "Between a Dog and a Green Space: Applying Ecosystem Services Theory to Explore the Human Benefits of Off-the-Leash Parks," *Landscape Research* 45, no. 2 (January 2020): 81–82.

9 Kirk Varnedoe and Adam Gopnik, *High and Low: Modern Art and Popular Culture*, New York: Museum of Modern Art, 1990, p. 18.

10 Clement Greenberg, "Avant-Garde and Kitsch," in *Art and Culture: Critical Essays*, Boston: Beacon, 1961, p. 10.

11 This formalism was Greenberg's project, a project which has had more than a few detractors, who view painting, and art, as having a far broader purview—among them art as a political or social force that engages the world more aggressively.

fronting the New York Public Library on Fifth Avenue, figures long beloved in their respective cityscapes. Why might these be regarded more kindly as art than the dogs of Berczy Park? Is the issue, then, the realistic painting of the dogs retained from their origins as small toy figures?

To a large degree, yes. Enacted in stone, we read the beasts as "lions," but we also read them as "sculpture." We should recall, however, that sculpture from certain ancient cultures we hold in high regard, the Hellenistic Greek, for example, were originally polychromed in a manner we might today deem completely inappropriate. In reviewing a recent exhibition of sculptures of the human body, the critic Peter Schjeldahl noted that "painted sculpture, which had been common in medieval churches, dwindled to the margins of vulgar use, such as in carnivals and religious processions, and decorative embellishment, as with ceramic figurines."[12] Accustomed as we are to seeing timeworn figures from ancient cultures as white, cream, or gray, this revelation may come as a bit of a shock. That these realistically painted figures may be troublesome, Schjeldahl explains, derives from a "resilient compound, in élite culture, of Platonic idealism and run-of-the-mill snobbery."[13] Perhaps so.

Instead, we prefer the chiseled and smooth stone surfaces of classical sculpture left monochrome, although we may now know that at the time of their creation this was not the case. Perhaps, the Berczy dogs will also fade over time and approach a monochromatic state; after all, municipal governments have not been famous for expending their limited financial resources on such specialized maintenance, and the winters of Toronto are hardly benign. But for now, however, the painting is trompe l'œil, and from afar it impresses visitors with its look of absolute reality. With lifelike rendering we read the dogs as dogs rather than as sculpture, and to many—at least to many in the art world, and perhaps some in the landscape profession as well—that is what renders the fountain and its dogs as kitsch, sentimentally tugging on visitor emotions. While one may or may not agree with this judgment, we can nonetheless look at the effect of the work rather than its formal attributes. Perhaps an appropriate summation of popular reaction to the Berczy fountain is conveyed in a statement by Jeff Koons regarding his own sculpture: "I've tried to make work that any viewer, no matter where they came from, would have to respond to, would have to say that on some level, 'Yes, I like it.' If they couldn't do that, it would only be because they had been told they were not supposed to like it. Eventually they will strip all that down and say, 'You know, it's silly, but I like that piece. It's great.'"[14]

021
Jeff Koons.
Balloon Dog (Magenta),
1994-2000.
Palazzo Grassi, Venice, Italy.
[© Jeff Koons]

022
Martha Schwartz.
Rio Shopping Center landscape.
Atlanta, Georgia, 1988.
[© Martha Schwartz Partners]

By commandeering known objects for his work—in this case, realistic toy dogs—Cormier has created his own "ready-mades," an art status granted to common objects recontextualized by Marcel Duchamp early in the twentieth century. Rather than requiring any significant alteration of form, Duchamp asserted that the artist's intention and the change of context alone could elevate and shift the object's category from ubiquitous to artistic. Duchamp famously displayed a common urinal and claimed its status as an artwork at the exhibition of the Society of Independent Artists in 1917. He dubbed the piece *Fountain*. At Cormier's own fountain, the dog supplies the water rather than consumes it; the arrangement and stacking of the animals and their overall number are hardly those found in the world of nature.[15] Is this not the hallmark of an artwork? Cormier makes no claims that his projects are art, unlike Martha Schwartz, whose landscape designs have often aspired to that status. Instead, Cormier addresses functional, social, and environmental issues with a serious demeanor, even if the resulting end product may be read as fun. Schwartz's grid of golden frogs at the Rio Shopping Center in Atlanta, or the mirror balls at the Center for Innovative Technology in Herndon, Virginia, or her Plexiglas structures at the housing in Gifu, Japan, are primarily visual, taken by some as beautiful and intriguing [**022**]. Ultimately, however, they all do provide at least limited physical comfort, even if geared more to the mind than the body.[16] Cormier's landscapes, in contrast, almost always provide a superstructure or keel that grounds the design in a traditional practice guided by a conscious regard for client, place, and budget.

Perhaps it is the landscape designs and installations by Ken Smith, also a former Martha Schwartz associate, that most closely parallel those of Cormier. Works such as the pinwheel installation *Daisy Border*—like Cormier's *Blue Tree*, also installed at Cornerstone Gardens in Sonoma, California—more closely parallels Schwartz

12 Peter Schjeldahl, "'Like Life' Shows Seven Hundred Years of the Body," *New Yorker*, 2 April 2018, https://www.newyorker.com/magazine/2018/04/02/like-life-shows-seven-hundred-years-of-the-body.

13 Ibid.

14 Quoted in Arthur C. Danto, "Banality and Celebration: The Art of Jeff Koons," in *Jeff Koons: Retrospektiv/Retrospective*, edited by Marit Woltmann, Oslo: Astrup Fearnley Museum of Modern Art, 2004, p. 130.

15 As a source of liquid, the dog usually emits it from the other end of its body.

16 Marc Treib, "A Constellation of Pieces," *Landscape Architecture* (March 2002): 58–67. Of late, Schwartz has turned her attention, at least in public presentations, to issues of climate change rather than art. See also *Martha Schwartz: Transfiguration of the Commonplace*, Washington, D.C.: Spacemaker, 1996; and Tim Richardson, ed., *The Vanguard Landscapes and Gardens of Martha Schwartz*, London: Thames & Hudson, 2004.

in that this particular piece was made only to delight, by profiting from the strong winds that frequently blow across the site [023]. In other projects, however, the playful dimension is less evident, for example in Smith's 2009 community gardens at Bedford–Stuyvesant in Brooklyn, or his 2006 design for the conversion of a former military base into the Orange County Great Park in Irvine, California.[17] In these later projects other parameters have prevailed; for example, in the latter design, social concerns and the colossal dimensions of the existing runways dictated an approach and elements more characteristic of normal landscape practice. It becomes obvious

023
Ken Smith.
Daisy Border, 2004.
Cornerstone Festival of Gardens,
Sonoma, California.
[Marc Treib]

that for Cormier it is not a question of being serious or having fun: it is possible to have both, although the balance of considerations from one to the other will vary with the client, budget, and task at hand. The singer Dolly Parton once instructed us to "find out who you are and do it on purpose."[18] Cormier seems to have found out who he is and executes his projects on purpose, and with a purpose.

There is little question that Berczy Park as a whole and its fountain in particular bring joyfulness to those who visit, whether the visitors possess four legs or but two. A smile often turns to laughter when someone encounters the sculptures and the play of water. I would venture that a touch of kitsch is unavoidable and inescapable given the realism of the figures. However, the act of transposing realistically rendered dogs into water sources in itself constitutes an act of appropriation and abstraction, as living canines rarely spout water at *that* end of their bodies with the same volume, vigor, and continuity—no matter how much water they may have ingested. The transposition from subject to source itself also represents a transformation that removes the work from any condemnation as kitsch, at least to any significant degree. Greenberg probably would not agree, however.

In several of his projects Cormier has purposely trod the narrow line between art and kitsch. In artworks, such as *Les Peluches* (Stuffed Animals), he has reveled in challenging the nature of that border—and, perhaps, has even stepped over it [024]. With fourteen other artists and designers, Cormier was commissioned by the Montreal Museum of Fine Arts to create an artwork for its 2011 exhibition *Big Bang*. Each of the participants was invited

17 See *Ken Smith: Landscape Architect*, New York: Monacelli, 2009.

18 http://www.zimbio.com/Dolly+Parton/articles/PyO3dZ_Eqi/26+Dolly+Parton+Quotes+Prove+Cooler+Smarter.

024
Claude Cormier.
Les Peluches
(Stuffed Animals).
Montreal Museum of Fine Arts.
Montréal, Québec, 2011.
[Natasha Gysin]

to select a piece from the museum's collection and have their new artwork engage it in dialog. In response, the landscape architect formulated a relief of monumental proportions (some eight by sixteen feet), a wall-size three-dimensional carpet comprised of small stuffed animals supposedly configured to address a twelfth-century *Head of an Apostle*. Cormier's self-imposed constraints dictated that the toys should all be at least secondhand, secured only from thrift shops, and cost no more than three dollars Canadian. In relatively short order he amassed a gathering of animals that Noah would have envied, although they were neither collected, nor assembled, two by two. Instead, the soft relief comprised of some 3,500 stuffed animals, all quite cute, visually blasted unsuspecting museumgoers as they left the elevator on the museum's second floor. It still does. The work was an instant hit, and virtually no one can resist taking a selfie while posing against the background of ingratiating little animals of diverse colors and species.

Again, the question of kitsch arises. At what point do "cute" and "crowd-pleasing" turn to true kitsch? In painting, for example, animals used as human surrogates trace back at least to the Renaissance. In their early appearances, moral or allegorical intentions may have instigated the substitution of animal forms for those human, although many allegories were also accompanied by an element of play and humor. However, in paintings from the centuries that followed, such as the 1894 *A Friend in Need*, one suspects that the artist's intention behind depicting a pack of card-playing dogs was purely to create a laugh, perhaps abetted by a mild touch of sarcasm in the rendering of the subject matter [025].[19] In this canine edition, common card play provokes questions: Can dog paws really hold a "hand" of cards? Can dogs really make decisions about holding and folding?[20] In all, just how *could* they? This series of dog paintings by Cassius Marcellus Coolidge has more than once served as an example of kitsch by those who argue against it: the diminution of seriousness and meaning through irony and humor, achieved by replacing human actors with their animal proxies. Kitsch, Winfried Menninghaus declares, "offers instantaneous emotional gratification without intellectual effort, without the requirement of distance, without sublimation."[21] Admittedly, appreciating the humor of card-playing dogs requires little intellectual achievement; it is in fact just a gag—although in earlier times such animal transpositions may have served as acerbic comments on human behavior. But what about the full-scale dogs that animate that fountain in Toronto?

For one, in the case of the Berczy fountain—and for most popular imagery used in landscape architecture—our experience is multisensory and not exclusively visual. A painting possesses only two dimensions; in contrast, a landscape is three-dimensional and is experienced through a fourth dimension of time and movement. While some might argue that canine realism diminishes the degree of one's intellectual engagement, in the case of the Berczy fountain one cannot dismiss the amenity of sound, spray, and animation that it provides—and in this case, the charm offered by a pack of water-spewing dogs. We are all well aware that nothing loses its punch more quickly than an old joke, or falls as flat as humor whose effect hinges on an unfamiliar reference. These were the principal problems that plagued the use of irony and historical references in postmodern architecture during the 1970s and 1980s.[22] While a sly insider architectural reference to Balthasar Neumann's 1772 Vierzehnheiligen Church in Staffelstein, Germany, may require some explanation, no one needs to "explain" a dog. Henry David Thoreau once quipped: "Some circumstantial evidence is very strong, as when you find a trout in the milk." Or a dog

025
Cassius Marcellus Coolidge. *A Friend in Need*, 1903. [Wikimedia Commons, Public Domain]

in your fountain. Is it not possible to enjoy a place *both* physically and mentally? Is there not a place for humor in our living environment? Or does any popular image or realistically rendered canine immediately relegate the work to the status of kitsch? Even so, kitsch does provide real enjoyment for a considerable segment of the audience.

Some artworks can succeed as art both fine and popular; in fact, one might argue, as did Varnedoe and Gopnik, that the distinction between the two categories no longer holds. Since the arrival of Pop Art in the 1960s, we have come to accept the appearance of everyday culture granted display in art museums. Whether a comic-book image painted large by Roy Lichtenstein, an electric fan rendered soft in a work by Claes Oldenburg, or more recently a "balloon dog" enlarged by Jeff Koons and fabricated in candy-colored stainless steel, the quotidian world has long been accepted as content by the world of high art. Varnedoe and Gopnik cite some Koons works as puerile in their forms and intentions, "But now puerility [is] in dialogue with the look of the cold luxury object."[23] The artist has said that "I wanted them to be irresistible, to get you on every level," an intention possibly shared by Cormier.[24] As cited previously, in certain early works Koons reversed the artistic trajectory used by Oldenburg and his predilection for reinterpreting in pliable materials the stiff forms of common objects. In contrast, Koons rendered rigid inflatable bunnies or balloons by casting them in stainless steel, either at true or enlarged dimensions. Koons has gone even further, however, enlarging the form of a small puppy into a monumental living work sheathed with flowering plants. Although other works by the artist have been condemned as kitsch or vulgar, I have found no similar attack on *Puppy,* a version of which remains on view in front of

19 *Dogs Playing Poker*, by Cassius Marcellus Coolidge, refers collectively to an 1894 painting, a 1903 series of sixteen oil paintings commissioned by Brown & Bigelow to advertise cigars, and a 1910 painting. All eighteen paintings in the series feature anthropomorphized dogs, but those in which dogs are seated around a card table have become well known in the United States as examples of home decoration branded as kitsch.

20 See (or hear) Kenny Rogers's hit song *The Gambler*, written by Don Schlitz and released in 1978. The refrain includes the lines "You got to know when to hold 'em / Know when to fold 'em / Know when to walk away / And know when to run."

21 Winfried Menninghaus, "On the Vital Significance of 'Kitsch': Walter Benjamin's Politics of 'Bad Taste'" (2009). In Andrew Benjamin and Charles Rice, eds., *Walter Benjamin and the Architecture of Modernity*, Melbourne: re.press, 2016, pp. 39–58.

22 During the 1960s, humor, irony, and references to past architecture were a significant aspect of the work of Venturi and Rauch, among other architects. See: Robert Venturi, *Complexity and Contradiction in Architecture*, New York: Museum of Modern Art, 1966.

23 Varnedoe and Gopnik, *High and Low*, p. 396.

24 Ibid., quoted on p. 396. Jeff Koons in conversation with Varnedoe and Gopnik, February 1989.

the Museo Guggenheim Bilbao, Spain [026].[25] Virtually every visitor postpones his or her entry into the museum by heading straight to *Puppy*, a must-use background for a selfie. *Puppy* succeeds because its form, while recognizable, is sufficiently abstract to be accepted as art. Further accessibility derives from its rendition in colorful living materials. One may take *Puppy* as sculpture, or perhaps even as a garden. After all, Koons's works are found within museums as well as outside them.

I don't find Claude Cormier's projects, even the more extreme designs like the Berczy fountain, to be kitsch—too much substance lies behind both the thinking and the realization of the work, both bolstered by the amenity the fountain provides. On the other hand, some might read the park as an exercise in *camp*, a term today somewhat out of vogue and favor but still circulating in certain aesthetic and cultural circles. We might say that if kitsch represents a denigration of an idea or artwork, camp is more the celebration of an exaggerated form or social behavior. In her classic 1964 essay "Notes on 'Camp'" the literary and film critic Susan Sontag qualified the term as involving a "theatricalization of experience," often accompanied by a sense of wit. It is a sensibility rather than an idea, and it involves "artifice and exaggeration," and among other aspects "converts the serious into the frivolous."[26] "Nothing in nature can be campy."[27] And yet despite this seeming, if light, condemnation, we might agree that there is a place for camp in our lives, and by extension, also in our public spaces. Sontag adds, "It is the love of the exaggerated, the 'off,' of things-being-what-they-are not," which might also be taken as one definition, or at least role, of art.[28] So then, might the dogs in Berczy Park qualify as art, or only camp?

It seems clear that the Berczy fountain and its dogs have been made to amuse and enchant, perhaps by adding a lighter moment to a heavy workday or relief from personal cares. While it's a fun work, this is serious fun—which may also be regarded as camp. Sontag again: "In naïve, or pure, Camp, the essential element is seriousness, a seriousness that fails. Of course, not all seriousness that fails can be redeemed as Camp. Only that which has the proper mixture of the exaggerated, the fantastic, the passionate, and the naïve."[29] Let us parse her qualifications of camp. The treatment of the dogs has been exaggerated in color perhaps, but not in size, which is accurate. The agglomeration of canines and their composition are certainly fantastic, but the care behind the design and construction of the work demonstrates a passion for the project that can't be denied. The fountain and the park do not comprise a naïve

026
Jeff Koons.
Puppy, 1992.
Guggenheim Museum,
Bilbao, Spain.
© Jeff Koons
© FMGB Guggenheim Bilbao
[Image source: Guggenheim
Bilbao Museoa,
photo by Erika Barahona Ede]

production because every one of its aspects, whether formal or social, has been carefully considered, shaped, and resolved. There is no attempt to falsify seriousness; this is real seriousness. "One can be serious about the frivolous," Sontag notes, "and frivolous about the serious," attitudes that may have passed through Cormier's mind at different stages of the project.[30] Seriousness and fun should not be taken as always antithetical; even fun can be serious. Fun or not, the park provides fresh air and various amenities for relaxation and exercise. Those who do not care for the dogs, some cat lovers, for example, may still enjoy the cooling effect of the spray, as might others who pass by or linger amidst the greenery. Sontag admits that "there are other creative sensibilities besides the seriousness (both tragic and comic) of high culture and of the high style of evaluating people. And we cheat ourselves, as human beings, if we respect only the style of high culture, whatever else we may do or feel on the sly."[31] That is to say, there is a place for delight even if it has been contrived by popular themes or imagery.

Pop Art treated the objects of everyday life as worthy subjects for art. Transformed by the artist into the painted image or soft sculptural form, or granted a monumental scale far beyond the ordinary, the common object might then be regarded as high art. Once granted status as art and displayed in a museum, the referent objects will be viewed in a different light.[32] After seeing them as the subjects of Andy Warhol's sculptures or paintings, we may never regard the true Brillo box or the can of Campbell's soup in quite the same way. Our vision, and the meaning of the objects, have been changed through their artistic re-presentation.

In the 1960s, Pop Art mounted a frontal assault on abstraction and painting as personal expression, challenging the dominance of Abstract Expressionism by ranking imagery over gesture and artistic independence. Pop Art replaced pure abstraction with a return to figuration, adopting the most ordinary objects, graphic images, or situations as its subject matter. As a result, art appeared to be more accessible to a broader audience. Earlier, in 1955, the cultural historian Russell Lynes codified taste, and ultimately personal sensibility, as being highbrow, middlebrow, or lowbrow. Highbrow described the province of the wealthy and the intelligentsia, lowbrow the working classes, and middlebrow, well, somewhere in between. "The real highbrow's way of life," Lynes asserted, "is as intellectualized as his way of thinking, and as carefully plotted. He is likely to be either extremely self-conscious about his physical surroundings and creature comforts or else sublimely, and rather ostentatiously, indifferent to them."[33] Although the highbrow might disdain, for example, the use of dogs as sources for a fountain, Lynes suggests that a shared affinity exists between the highbrow and lowbrow, although their values ultimately relate at divergent levels. For example,

25 Koons created a second vegetal work, *Split-Rocker* (2000), which joined the heads of two giant rocking horses executed in flowers and plants. In this piece, however, the form is more difficult to discern and therefore exerts less of an impact.

26 Sontag, "Notes on 'Camp,'" 1964, reprinted in Sontag, *Against Interpretation*, p. 275.

27 Ibid., p. 279.

28 Ibid.

29 Ibid., p. 283.

30 Ibid., p. 288.

31 Ibid., pp. 286–87.

32 This idea of transposition, or the erasure of the distinction between so-called high and low culture, also applies to the work of the Japanese artist Takashi Murakami. "What Murakami perceived as a revival of artisan traditions and a refusal of Western conceptions of 'high' and 'low' could be read as Pop nihilism in the US, where vast audiences could enjoy his colorful work without worrying about the backstory." William S. Smith, "The Weak and the Dead: What the Rise of KAWS Says about the Art World's Ailments," *Art in America* (September 2019), p. 61.

33 Russell Lynes, *The Tastemakers: The Shaping of American Popular Taste*, New York: Harper and Brothers, 1955; reprint, New York: Dover, 1980, p. 315.

the highbrow can appreciate jazz, which Lynes considered essentially lowbrow terrain. It is the middlebrow whom Lynes casts as the threat to the highbrow, given their pretense and use of "culture to satisfy social or business ambitions."[34] Virginia Woolf was incensed that her writing might be taken as middlebrow because to her such a categorization signified that her work was not of the highest quality. In a letter never sent to the *New Statesman and Nation* she wrote, "If any human being, man, woman, dog, cat, or half-crushed worm dares call me 'middlebrow' I will take my pen and stab him dead."[35] One assumes this was written with humor as well as righteous indignation. In contrast, Lynes believed that the lowbrow "wants to be comfortable and to enjoy himself without having to worry about whether he has good taste or not."[36] So just where does taste lie, and how can we apply such thinking to projects comprised of pink plastic balls, magenta tree trunks, or multicolored temporary road markers? While today we might seek to make art accessible to broader audiences through schoolchildren tours and museum outreach programs, to a large extent the content of art has remained consistently highbrow. Pop Art was an exception, as was folk art before it, having been created within the community itself. In this respect we might read even the most extreme of Cormier's work as "all-brow," regarded by many in the highbrow community as art (admittedly with a wink or a grimace), and middle- and lowbrow in terms of its broad appeal. "We need some measure of sentimentality and the ennoblement of old kitsch in a new way," claimed the Austrian-born architect and designer Josef Frank.[37] That is to say, there should be something for everyone, and everyone can read that something as she or he likes.

Art Installations

To a degree unusual in landscape architectural practices, Claude Cormier has maintained a continuing involvement with installations of limited duration that have served as research for design. Whether these merit the term "art" or "design" is left to the individual—Cormier himself makes no such claim—but these projects have provided him with the opportunities for morphological and experiential investigations that landscape architecture commissions often preclude. When conceiving an installation, the designer can choose to discard the restrictions imposed by the host of parameters that usually constrain landscape commissions and instead select only one or several factors to generate the idea for the work. With work that is temporary one can take greater risks; being regarded as artworks grants the designer the freedom to avoid

027
Gertrude Jekyll. Hestercombe. Taunton, England, ca. 1904. The pergola with borders. [Marc Treib]

issues of function and, at least to some degree, liability. These projects also furnish the Cormier team with a freer hand to inject greater degrees of irony and humor into its work, mental dimensions that might not be typical, say, of the landscape for a developer's condominium apartment tower. An early installation, at the Métis Garden Festival in northern Québec, replaced living plant materials with painted wooden sticks, as Cormier believed that the limited time provided for planting and growth would be insufficient to yield the horticultural effects he desired. Interestingly, in describing the project in a 2015 lecture at the Gardner Museum in Boston, Cormier cited the color investigations of the celebrated British garden designer Gertrude Jekyll as his point of departure for the installation at Métis.[38] Jekyll is known for herbaceous borders marked by an abundance of color and textural richness, and equally for an artistic practice supported by her encyclopedically scientific knowledge of plants, their physical characteristics, colors, and most of all, their growth and duration [027]. Acknowledging that the time constraints imposed on him at Métis would preclude any significant horticultural invention, Cormier instead turned to lumber roughly two inches square in section.

The generating idea for the installation was to create another type of "border," this one composed not with flowers but with wooden posts: masses, swaths of painted posts [028]. Colored blue on three sides, when viewed from one direction the field of posts would appear blue—in reference to the Himalayan blue poppy, for which the estate garden at Métis is known—tinting the walkway with an effect not unlike that of a mass of bluebells or lupine [029]. Only three sides of the sticks were painted blue, however; the remaining side was painted international orange in reference to the color at the center of the poppy. Approached from one end of the rectangular field occupied by the installation the meadow of painted sticks appeared to be completely blue [030]. As the visitors walked through the installation, however, the color field shifted from one hue to the other, with a mix of blue and orange as the transitional reading, ultimately appearing all orange. After its successful appearance at Métis, *Blue Stick Garden* was subsequently installed at Hestercombe in Taunton, England, the site of one of the most impressive of Jekyll's gardens—a garden recreated from scratch during the 1980s. This "second coming" of *Blue Stick Garden* represented an acknowledgment of both the Jekyll references used by Cormier in generating the installation, and the positive reception it first received by the Canadian garden public as well as Métis's British visitors.[39]

A notable gap divides the Cormier installations at garden shows and those appearing as urban interventions. Visitors to garden shows attend by choice; in the city, any work is open to comprehensive public scrutiny and criticism. Interwoven with the Cormier garden show and sculpture installations are the landscape architectural commissions at the heart of the office's practice, urban projects that respond to and address the specific conditions of the site. Unlike the landscape projects, the Cormier installations have

34 Ibid., p. 313.

35 Virginia Woolf, published posthumously in the *Death of the Moth and Other Essays*, quoted in Hana Leaper, "Opinion: 'Middlebrow' Art," *Tate Etc.* (Spring 2018), p. 24.

36 Lynes, p. 319.

37 Josef Frank, "What Is Modern?" 1930, cited in Alan Powers, *The Bauhaus Goes West: Modern Art and Design in Britain and America*, London: Thames & Hudson, 2019, p. 255.

38 Claude Cormier, lecture, Isabella Stewart Gardner Museum, Boston, 22 September 2015.

39 Alas, while there was funding to bring the work to England from its original showing at Métis, there was no money for its return. After its demounting at Hestercombe, pieces of the installation appeared in many gardens around Taunton. Cormier, "Serious Fun," lecture.

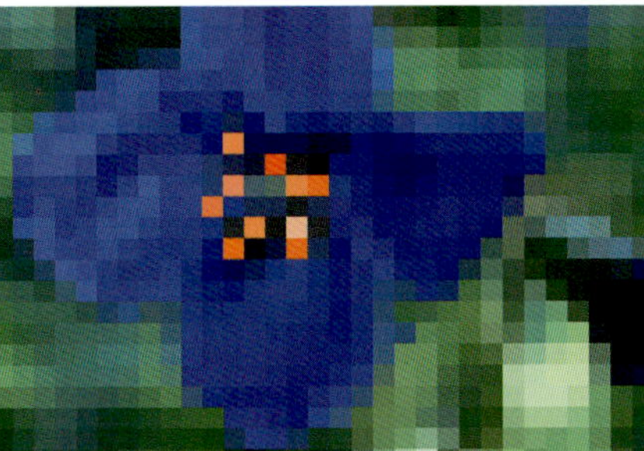

028
(above)
Blue Stick Garden.
Métis-sur-Mer, Québec,
2000+.
The sticks seen
from the blue side.
[Claude Cormier
et Associés]

029
(center)
Blue Stick Garden.
Abstraction of
blue poppies.
[Louise Tanguay,
Claude Cormier
et Associés]

030
(opposite)
Blue Stick Garden.
[Louise Tanguay]

031
(left)
Blue Stick Garden.
Old Port, Montréal,
Québec, 2012.
Here, the work occupies
a traffic circle.
[Marc Cramer]

tended to rely on synthetic rather than living materials, with binary color play recurring as a key component of the designs. Over the years since the original installation, stick works derived from the Métis piece have appeared in several locations, among them a circular mass of similar narrow posts that occupies the center of the roundabout in Montréal's Old Port, whose origin accompanied the development of Cormier's Clock Tower Beach project discussed below [031]. In this particular location, the perception of the colors changes as one circles the roundabout, unlike at Métis where the shift derived exclusively from the direction of one's walk.

In a different guise, color pairing reappeared in the multiyear series of four installations on the avenue du Musée in Montréal, a street flanked on either side by the buildings of the Montreal Museum of Fine Arts. In these installations, Cormier profited from the flexibility, economy, and chromatic properties of the "temporary overlay marker," or TOM—those small plastic flaps used in roadwork to provisionally mark vehicle lanes before more permanent lines are painted on the road surface. Configured as geometric patterns with varying degrees of rigor and fluidity, the patterns of these temporary installations were meant to be agreeable when seen from ground level as well as from above—from the windows of the museum's main building across the street, for example. Since their initial showing in summer 2013, Cormier has installed four different iterations on the street, which is closed to traffic for just this purpose during the summer months. *TOM I* took a field of daisies as its inspiration—using some 3,000 tabs, primarily yellow and white—whose chromatic reading, once again, shifted with the position of the visitors as they approached or departed from the museum [032]. *TOM II* relied instead on a painting, in this case Vincent van Gogh's *Field with Poppies* (ca. 1890) as its point of departure, and proposed a mixed ground of seemingly randomly-arranged splotches of green and red that could be interpreted as a geometrized meadow of white and yellow double daisies. *TOM III* appeared as a singular figure more rigorously unified, although it employed the same logic and color shifts characteristic of the earlier editions. Reading the arena of 12,000 TOMs from straight on, laterally, or diagonally yielded differing alignments and revelations of color, convincingly demonstrating that simple forms can nonetheless produce complex perceptual results. In contrast to the chevron ordering of the prior summer, the 2017 edition of *TOM IV* interwove spirals and radial figures that generated mixes of colors, morphing continually as one passed through them [033]. To some visitors, perhaps the array of flexible rectangular plastic tabs was perceived as a meadow filled with flowers, like one that might have existed in the two-dimensional world Edwin A. Abbott described in his 1884 science fiction novel *Flatland*.[40] When viewed from above, this last installation—the volume of whose medium had grown to 15,000 tabs—lacked visual coherence as an overall figure and was more engaging when experienced from the ground as individual sections [034]. As the TOM plastic tabs are flexible and tough—after all, they are made to resist the weight of the automobiles and trucks that pass over them—visitors have been invited to traverse the installations as well as view them from above and afar. The smiles on the faces of the children who followed the lines and curves, or who tried their very best to stomp on and squash them, underscore the appeal of these installations, and transformed this particular iteration into a Field of Screams (of delight, of course) [035].

40 Edwin A. Abbott, *Flatland: A Romance of Many Dimensions*, London: Seeley, 1884.

032
TOM I.
Montreal Museum
of Fine Arts.
Montréal, Québec, 2012.
[Guillaume Paradis,
Claude Cormier
et Associés]

033
TOM IV.
Montreal Museum
of Fine Arts.
Montréal, Québec, 2017.
TOM detail, new colors.
[Guillaume Paradis,
Claude Cormier
et Associés]

034
TOM IV.
Montreal Museum
of Fine Arts.
Montréal, Québec, 2017.
Circles and radiating lines.
[Marc Treib]

035
TOM IV.
Montreal Museum
of Fine Arts.
An appreciative audience.
[Marc Treib]

Balls (Les Boules)

To the citizens of Montréal, the series of temporary vaulted canopies installed over rue Sainte-Catherine Est is probably Cormier's best-known and certainly most-publicized work. The intention behind the project was to inject life in a rundown area of the city plagued by drug use, property vacancies, and a high degree of homelessness. It is also a district with a major gay population and is often referred to as Montréal's "Gay Village." Behind the project was the intention to inject new life into the quarter by shining a spotlight upon it, thereby attracting more people to the neighborhood in order to increase commerce and stabilize the declining social milieu. The budget was limited. The challenge: How to transform a derelict neighborhood using only simple means, on a single—though one-kilometer long—street with an intervention supported by very limited funds. The solution: balls. Plastic balls, to be more precise, balls not unlike those used to sheathe the *Blue Tree* at Cornerstone a decade before, and those used at an art biennial held by the city of Le Havre, France, in 2006 [**036**]. There, Cormier used multicolored plastic balls as surrogates for the flowers and leaves missing on several of the city's monumental pergolas—in a sense, using synthetic components to compensate for the missing vegetation. But unlike in Le Havre, here in Montréal there would be balls of only one color, and that color would be pink. Cormier's first use of plastic and balls in an intervention had not been pink, however, but light blue.

Cornerstone Gardens and Marketplace was envisioned as a private garden festival paired with a small commercial center set along a major highway in southern Sonoma County in Northern California. In its initial year, 2004, the sponsor invited sixteen landscape architects to create installations on a site retrieved from prior agricultural use. Like several garden shows that preceded it, the master plan for the Cornerstone Festival of Gardens assigned small plots for each of the participant's gardens, with little restriction on their content or look, other than budget and the requirement for a reasonable amount of technology for construction and maintenance. In response to these directives, Cormier again took an oblique turn from a typical garden. Rather than designing a garden enclosed by a green hedge like the others at the festival, he proposed to recast an existing tree, a moribund Monterey pine slated for removal. Using the analogy of an object in a photograph digitally erased using Photoshop, Cormier proposed to visually "remove" the tree by matching its new color with that of an idealized, always blue, Sonoma sky. In other words, by coloring the tree blue, its identity could be masked, much in the manner of camouflage—only in this case the camouflage would be a monochromatic azure possessing no pattern. The medium of transfiguration would be light blue plastic balls affixed to the trunk and branches of the tree after it had been pruned to yield a more agreeable shape and manageable volume. Of the 100,000 plastic balls ordered at 8 cents per unit, some 80,000 were actually installed; a cherry picker was used to mount the balls, strung on wires, on the upper trunk and branches [**037**]. This was indeed a curious gesture, this encrustation of a natural form with light-blue plastic barnacles; in some ways the gesture was more than slightly perverse. But it was also the *perfect* gesture, perfect in its inserting a striking vertical element into an essentially horizontal landscape. Like the *flèche* of a Gothic cathedral, the blue tree joined ground and sky—or was it Earth and Heaven? Perhaps. Despite any possible condemnation, *Blue Tree* unquestionably provided Cornerstone with a center point, even a campanile, that marked its location and announced its presence to those passing by on California State Route 121. Although

036
Pergola installation.
Le Havre's Contemporary Art Biennial.
Le Havre, France, 2006.
[Jacques Perron]

037
Blue Tree.
Cornerstone Festival of Gardens.
Sonoma, California, 2004.
Detail.
[David Aquilina]

038
(opposite)
Pink Balls.
Montréal, Québec, 2011.
Street view.
[Marc Cramer]

STELLA ARTOIS
VOTRE VIN
mozza

039
Pink Balls.
Montréal, Québec, 2011.
Lateral view accross
Sainte-Catherine Street
East.
[Marc Cramer]

projected to last only three months, the piece actually endured for about three years, at which time the blue of the plastic had faded drastically and the decayed condition of the tree beneath the balls had reached the point of no return. In response, both the balls and the tree were removed.

In a way similar to the twirling foil strips used by car dealers to define their lots and instigate sales, in Montréal the strings of pink plastic balls were configured to "roof" rue Sainte-Catherine Est and create a "vaulted nave" that surpassed in length even the grandest Gothic cathedral [**038**]. Because the installation was projected to endure for only the summer months, a system of structural supports was devised to keep each string of balls, which assumed a graceful catenary curve when draped, independent of the buildings on either side of the street. Unfortunately, the Chinese company that had supplied the balls for the *Blue Tree* installation could not meet the tight deadline needed to mount the project; instead, Cormier turned to a plastic-production company in Québec. The change in source, while solving one problem created another. Rather than receiving the balls assembled and complete with mounting pins, as they had for *Blue Tree* project, the balls would arrive in halves and require a massive number of hours for assembly. To meet this challenge both the process and nature of the project were immediately changed; now members of the community would assemble the 180,000 units—much in the communal manner of the barn raising or quilting bee of old—a social event that resulted in bringing the village, as well as the balls, together. One might even say that the volunteers and their community were joined by the balls. Installation along the street then proceeded, a process requiring some three weeks [**039**]. The result was spectacular but immediately, yet again, there was the question of Cormier's choice of color.

Blue was appropriate for joining tree and sky in Sonoma, but what color for Montréal's Gay Village? Pink seemed appropriate. Pink as a contrast against the sky, whether blue or gray? Pink for its stereotype of femininity, perhaps? Or was pink a queer marker that followed in the tradition of the pink AIDS triangle? Pink has reappeared as the color of choice for several Cormier projects that include the umbrellas at Sugar Beach and the *Lipstick Forest* at the Montréal Palais des congrès [**040**]. In the latter case, the color was suggested by the promotional campaign for the city that replaced the "o" in Montréal with the lipstick trace of a kiss—symbolizing love perhaps? Hence the lurid pink color, and hence the name *Lipstick Forest*. In other situations, however, the use of pink may just be the landscape architect's color preference or what was deemed a good choice for realizing the desired effect. As Freud is reported to have once said, sometimes a cigar is just a cigar; sometimes pink may just be the best choice of color, a choice made without consciously addressing questions of connotation.

The initial showing of *Pink Balls* was an unmitigated success, praised by the community, the city, and the press alike. The gently swaying "roof" over rue Sainte-Catherine Est added considerable life to the "village" and economic gain for the district. Within rather few years the vacancy rate for shops in the neighborhood dropped from 20 percent to 7 percent. During the summers when the balls cover the street, traffic is banned by day, and by night Sainte-Catherine Street East hosts a promenade of locals and visitors alike. Profiting from the increase in foot traffic, shops and restaurants opened or reopened and new life energized the street and the quarter. Of course, not every improvement to the social and economic environments of the district can be attributed to the *Pink Balls* project, but it certainly provided at catalyst to prime the pump.

040
Lipstick Forest.
Palais des congrès
de Montréal.
Montréal, Québec, 2002.
[Jean-François Vézina]

041
18 Shades of Gay.
Montréal, Québec, 2017.
The street in the city.
[www.ouramericandream.fr]

Like the TOM installations, what began as a one-off event, the return of the balls has become an annual festival. In 2017, after several returns of *Pink Balls*, Cormier reconceived the project and departed from the original monochrome to conjure a chromatic rainbow in the manner of the LGBTQ+ flag. This edition was appropriately named *18 Shades of Gay* [041] [042] [043]. Given the construction experience acquired over the years of the *Pink Balls*, the required installation time was reduced from the original three weeks to just five days. In this edition, weeping willows in planters, 150 in all, were positioned along the route. Drawn by the new chromatic variation and vibrancy, the crowds were even larger in 2017 than in prior years, and the number of programmed events greater. While essentially ornamentation at urban scale, the rue Sainte-Catherine Est project has nonetheless effected cultural and commercial change. Due to its continuing success, the installations endured, although Cormier has admitted that given the amount of time required and the strain he experienced annually, he was very relieved to put the project in other hands, which took place after its last installation in 2019. A competition has been held and a design selected, but when and if it will be realized is not known. But it is always difficult to turn the reins over to others when one has already invested so much in the project. Until now, however, rue Sainte-Catherine Est remains Cormier's most rewarding burden, balls and all.

There is little doubt of the theatrical aspect accompanying many of these art projects, installations, and landscapes: the grove of lipstick-pink trees in the Montréal Palais des congrès, the TOM configurations for the art museum, and of course the dog fountain at Berczy Park. If, as Shakespeare wrote, "all the world's a stage," Cormier contributes to our quotidian theater with décor, both living and inanimate—but with décor that surpasses mere decoration. Each of these installations became a stage that contributed to the life of the city, whether that life was playful, somber, or pragmatic. To regard the playful aspects as the only contribution of these landscapes, however, would be to sell them short as vehicles of life support and social and economic change—purposes they sustain in most admirable ways.

Urban interventions designed by the Cormier office have continued, for example, as the *Balade pour la Paix* that in 2017 occupied rue Sherbrooke between the Montreal Museum of Fine Arts to the west and the McGill University campus to the east [044]. Celebrating the simultaneous 375th anniversary of the city, the 150th anniversary of the establishment of the nation, and the 50th anniversary of Expo 67, the *Balade* displayed the flags of the world's nations, arranging them in alphabetical order from west to east.[41] By including the flags of all nations—a gesture inspired by Expo 67—Cormier hoped that the installation might even bring people together in this era of divisiveness.

The *Balade* project represents Cormier in a restrained mode. The character of rue Sherbrooke changes significantly along its length. In some places the street is flanked by tall buildings set flush to the street, while on other blocks they retreat behind a forecourt or garden. Significant differences in building styles and materials also characterize the architecture along the length of this, one of Montréal's major boulevards. Add to that the constraints imposed by a low budget, bus traffic, streetlamps, storms, signage, parking, and other elements of urban infrastructure—this was a civic and aesthetic intervention plagued by complexity. Twenty-nine sculptures selected by the art museum curators accompanied the parade of flags

41 Accompanied by outdoor sculpture.

042
18 Shades of Gay.
Montréal, Québec, 2017.
Green into blue.
[Raphaël Thibodeau]

043
18 Shades of Gay.
Orange into yellow.
[Jean-Michael Seminaro]

044
(opposite left)
Balade pour la Paix.
Montréal, Québec, 2017.
[Jean-François Savaria]

045
(opposite right)
Balade pour la Paix.
Support.
[Marc Treib]

along the extent of the route. How could any sort of unity and sense of procession be achieved amid the architectural and urban cacophony by using only pieces of colored cloth? Functionally, the greatest issue facing the designers was how to support the 220 flags, set some twenty-three feet apart, without significant physical disruption to the existing architecture and cityscape? In addition, all construction was required to be removed at the end of the celebration without leaving any noticeable trace. Working with industrial designer Michael Dallaire, Cormier devised what is essentially a steel tripod with one extended leg [**045**]. Mastaba-like concrete bases with battered sides provided sufficient weight to sustain the flagstaffs even in severe weather. Prefabricated of concrete and steel, the tripods provided a simple and elegant solution to a rather complex problem. Where these masts proved impractical, in certain segments of the route, cables substituted for the heavier supports. The effect of the *Balade*, as originally envisioned by its designers, was transformative and during the months of its presence rue Sherbrooke was alive with the color and movement of flags.

"Serious" Landscapes

Although Claude Cormier et Associés may be better known for their more imageable landscapes like the beaches and installations discussed within, these projects represent only one side of their practice. Other designs, though more quiet in aspect, possess an equal depth derived from the same intense reading of the physical and social conditions of the site. Of landscapes in this category, let us look at only three projects; others are discussed in detail in the accompanying essay by Susan Herrington. The place d'Youville in Montréal's historic quarter is long and narrow, with a width-to-length proportion of one-to-five in one section, and more than one-to-fifteen in another [**046**]. A sewer of considerable diameter beneath the median runs the full length of the street—a relic which has been determined to be of archeological interest. In response to these constraints, team Cormier initially proposed pouring a concrete slab to cap these subterranean features and protect them from intrusion. In recent memory the space has served as what is essentially a linear parking lot, with a complete lack of trees to soften the sense of closure generated by the blocks of heavy masonry buildings that flank the street on either side. Cormier's charge was to reinvigorate the place d'Youville, perhaps by reflecting the changing uses of the buildings along its length, perhaps by also helping stimulate a more vibrant social life. As in many other Cormier projects, the source of inspiration was an artwork, in this case one drawn from folk art: the crazy quilt. It is said that the design idea for quilts in this tradition was inspired by necessity, with their makers using whatever fabric remnant was at hand, no matter the size or shape. Although comprised of geometric forms, the seemingly random arrangement of the patchwork appeared irregular and without a governing order: in a word, "crazy."

Inspiration is one thing, the reality of a landscape design task yet another. Or as Confucius once put it, "When the wind stops, row"—at least Confucius as quoted in a graffito once seen on the walls of a Berkeley architecture school. In the case of place d'Youville, the design did not derive from any direct replication of the specific shapes used on any specific quilt, but from a logic derived from the play of oblique angles that characterized the shapes of the quilt's swatches.

In this case, the irregular shapes of which the quilt is composed suggested oblique lines that might connect the principal doorways of the buildings flanking the green space at the center of the elongated space. Realized in wood or stone of differing

046
(previous page)
Place d'Youville.
Montréal, Québec, 1999.
View from above.
[Denis Farley]

047
Place d'Youville.
Paving pattern showing
intersection of paths.
[Denis Farley]

types, sizes, shapes, and colors, these diagonal walkways intersect the main path that delineates the central spine of place d'Youville—albeit with some zigs, zags, and adjustments along the way necessitated by construction and the infrastructure along its length [047]. Vegetation plays only a supporting role, however, primarily as low shrubs cut into geometric masses that buffer the paths from the traffic lanes on either side of the walk and greenway.

In contrast to the place d'Youville, the scheme for the renovation of the place d'Armes, also in Montréal, proposed the retrieval of a historical structure long missing from the site [048].[42] The office had only a weekend to prepare the conceptual design, and from that point the city took over without any true additional input from the Cormier office. Given how few of their original ideas were eventually realized, Cormier is reluctant to even make any claim for the project other than for its generating ideas. Yet, despite this proviso, in its base concept, the place d'Armes proposal illustrates the office's use of history as a starting point for many of their landscape designs. Using historical documents, the Cormier team established the plan and position of the original église de Ville-Marie that occupied a site to the southeast of the present square. Treating the shape of the prior basilica's footprint as a wide and flat—and giant—speed bump, Cormier attempted to create a contemporary invocation of the historical church. Accompanying this ground-level element was the redesign of the place d'Armes itself, which in the end amounted to two linear flanks of elm trees that focus visitor attention on the church that replaced the historical basilica, much in the manner of the blinders used to keep an urban horse focused on the street ahead. An intricate pattern for the granite paving and an existing fountain accompanied the massed tree plantings. As it happens, the retrieval of the historical basilica was rejected by the Ministry of Culture and Communications, the Church, and the city, as was the cross—to be suspended in space and illuminated at night—intended to mark the cross that crowned the original steeple; thus, any suggestion of the historical basilica remained only as a proposal.

From the year of its inception centuries ago, Dorchester Square has served as one of the city's most active social hubs, attracting a broad cross-section of Québecois society and their guests. Even today one encounters a mélange of locals and tourists disposed around the square on benches or on the lawns [049]. The land that today comprises the square, as well as the place du Canada on the opposite side of boulevard René-Lévesque to its north, was originally a fragment of the cimetière Saint-Antoine that occupied the land from 1799 until 1854.[43] In that year the site's purpose turned from repose to more active use as a series of open spaces that in time became formalized as Dorchester Square. Inaugurated in 1878, but completed only in 1892, the original square featured more paving than planting, as greenery was relegated to several low planting beds lining the pathways [050]. Over time, a number of major commercial and religious buildings arose around the square, including the monumental St. George's Anglican Cathedral, opened in 1870, and the Windsor railroad station constructed on the south edge of the adjacent property at the close of the nineteenth century. At some time, but by 1907, pedestrian movement to and through the space was acknowledged in a revised layout of circulation paths whose pattern resembled that of the Union Jack. Later in the twentieth century, however, a segment of the site to the north was truncated by the construction of

42 In this instance, the scheme derived from a one-week competition.

43 https://en.wikipedia.org/wiki/Dorchester_Square.

048
(opposite)
Place d'armes.
Montréal, Québec, 2007.
Photomontage of design proposal.
[Claude Cormier et Associés]

049
Dorchester Square.
Montréal, Québec, 2010.
Mixed paving textures in dappled light.
[Raphaël Thibodeau]

050
Dorchester Square.
Montréal.
View ca. 1959.
[Source unknown]

the massive Dominion Building. The net effect was a composition spatially off-balanced, although the monument to the Boer War remained as its nominal center. Over the years the physical state of the square declined; its asphalt paths became cracked and chipped, and vegetation intruded on the right of way. In 2010 the city commissioned Claude Cormier et Associés to refurbish the square and restore its status as one of Canada's prime social spaces.[44]

The new design made no effort to erase all historical traces of the square's earlier states, nor to impose any new order alien to the site. Quite the contrary, in fact. The process was, instead, one of "find and replace"—and replace and elevate in subtle ways. The paths were retained in their existing configuration but were repaved with granite sets whose visual effect was enlivened by three degrees of roughness: thermal-finished, honed, and polished. The resulting "peppered" surface varies in its degree of visual sparkle under differing light conditions and with a shift of position as one moves through the square. Periodically, granite crosses have been inset into the field of granite sets as lithic recalls of the site's original use for burials [051].[45] As at Berczy Park the triangular lawn segments bounded by the pathways have been banked and softly modeled as low berms, thus giving volume to what originally was only a flat surface [052]. A similar strategy had been used in the earlier landscape for the Pierre-Dansereau Science Complex for the Université du Québec à Montréal, although in that project the "cellular" shapes of the mounds and the paths around them were more contemporary in form [053]. In the comprehensive reworking of Dorchester Square, whose initial study dates to 2005, the existing circulation network determined a series of elevated mounds whose volumes today define the two-dimensional paths of movement to the central monument and across the site. While subtle to an extreme, these resulting hillocks are nonetheless effective for defining the walkways and welcoming those who wish to sit or recline on a grassy surface. As an added benefit, the shallow mounds discourage the use of tents at events that often damage the lawns; their presence also discourages quotidian foot traffic by individuals and groups. The dark-gray granite curbs that edge each mound frame the grass panels distinguish them as distinct volumes, and may also be used for seating. More typically for restorations of this type, historical vegetation was replanted and once again today flowers encircle the square's monuments.

44 Cormier claims that circa 1900, Dorchester Square was the most important public space in Canada.

45 The small spur at the bottom of cross was taken from historical maps which used that form as a symbol for a cemetery.

051
Dorchester Square.
Montréal, Québec, 2010.
Paving detail showing
crosses and mixed
granite finishes.
[Raphaël Thibodeau]

40

052
(opposite)
Dorchester Square.
Montréal, Québec, 2010.
Banked mounds with
granite curbing.
[Raphaël Thibodeau]

053
Pierre-Dansereau
Science Campus,
Université du Québec
à Montréal, 2005.
Planters and mounds.
[Claude Cormier
et Associés]

The net effect of this restrained reworking is a landscape that feels the same, yet at the same time seems different, a landscape that expresses a comfortable continuity rather than an unsettling breach. Dorchester Square may be Cormier's most subtly designed and executed public landscape to date, and not incidentally his most sophisticated. In clement weather the square is usually filled with a healthy mix of people of all ages, sitting or reading on its benches or sprawling with lunch or a drink on one of its grassy banks. Whiffs of alcohol and marijuana may also enliven the air.[46]

In 2015 Cormier returned to Dorchester Square to realize the design for the adjacent parcel of the park to the north. The impetus was the planned revision to bus traffic on the site that in past years had narrowed the traffic lanes from six to two, and thus freed up land to augment the existing square [054]. Three pedestrian paths connect the old and new areas of the square: the first continues the principal axis of the park and aligns with the central corridor of the Dominion Building to the north; the remaining two paths have been graced with pedestrian bridges arched to allow auto access for the ramps entering and exiting the underground parking. On most days with pleasant weather the stepped bridges serve as much for, if not more for, seating as for passage [055]. Despite this additional parcel annexed to the square, there would nonetheless be insufficient space for the fountain proposed at an earlier date—jets and flowing water to add sparkle and ambient sound to the square's northern zone. Here the impish side of Cormier's thinking reappeared. Due to its projected weight and the presence of the parking garage below it, the proposed fountain required one of the garage's subterranean structural columns for support; as a result, the fountain's precise location was preordained. Due to the reduced surface area ultimately allotted to the fountain, however, space became insufficient for the erection of a complete fountain in the manner of, say, the one at Berczy Park. There was nothing to do, Cormier reasoned, other than to build only that part of the fountain that would fit on the condensed site. With a clean swipe—like a knife slicing through a wedding cake—one-third of the fountain was conceptually cut and removed [056]. The result does indeed provide a fountain for the Dorchester Square, with a shape, almost like one drawn in section, that faces the neighboring buildings. On its flat surface a realistically rendered woodpecker tries in vain to make an inroad into the fountain's cast-iron back surface. When presented to them, the Ministry of Culture was once again nervous about the Cormier proposal and how it would be received by the public. As for Cormier, he believes that, "if you are afraid [or nervous], it's probably the right decision."[47] While not as effective as the dog-and-water combo in Toronto, this bit of whimsy provides a welcome animation and a bit of humor to an otherwise staid, if very elegant, design.

In these three projects we see a conscious attempt to study history for ideas, not only for the present but also the future. The Cormier strategy eschews historicism and replication; his is a history abstracted, mined for inspiration, but completely reworked to function in today's city. The details and the selection of materials support and make concrete the driving concept. With the exception of the fountain at Dorchester Square, this is Cormier playing it straight, perhaps working as a landscape architect more typically does, but working with

46 The Cormier office also planned the revisions to the nearly adjacent place du Canada, which contains a central paved surface of a sizable area. The scheme, however, was executed by the Montréal parks department and the resulting landscape possesses less of the magic of the Dorchester Square.

47 Cormier, "Serious Fun," lecture.

054
Dorchester Square,
North Portion.
Montréal, Québec, 2018.
Plan.
[Claude Cormier
et Associés]

055
(overleaf)
Dorchester Square,
North Portion.
Pedestrian bridges
cross the entrance ramps
to underground parking.
[Jean-François Savaria]

peel pub
peel pub
SUBWAY

056
Dorchester Square.
Montréal, Québec, 2018.
Cartoon view.
[Cyril Doisneau]

an unusual degree of intelligence graced by an artistic touch. These works—and, of course, there are others—represent his restrained side, the side guided by a sense of what is appropriate, even if the resulting design at first appears to lack the imagery and immediate brilliance of the more witty schemes. In these works, the brilliance lies at a different level and appears in a different way, quietly, and with sophistication.

Establishing a Beachhead

Is it possible to create a place called a "beach" without a natural slope, sand, or even access to the water? Is it possible for a shoreline long dedicated to industrial use to offer any form of recreational amenity? And if so, can any such project contribute to a larger venture like the wholesale transformation of a former industrial lakeshore into a site for leisure activities? The series of "beaches" proposed—and mostly constructed—by Claude Cormier have addressed just these questions, each answer being affirmative, and at times achieving some rather spectacular results. To date there have been five such proposals; four have been realized.[48] Offering delight as well as respite, they are among Cormier's most triumphant and popular landscapes.

Where we stand, and what we see before us, significantly colors how we perceive places as well as the rewards we glean from them. At the beach, land and water meet: it is the end of one and the start of the other, but just which is which depends on where you stand and your state of mind, literally determining your "point of view." In *Invisible Cities*, Italo Calvino established how our reading of the city depends on our location and psychological condition. As they approach land, for example, sailors at sea perceive the imaginary city of Despina as a camel.

> *In the coastline's haze, the sailor discerns the form of a camel's withers, an embroidered saddle with glittering fringe between two spotted humps, advancing and swaying; he knows it is a city, but he thinks of it as a camel from whose pack hang wine-skins and bags of candied fruit, date wine, tobacco leaves, and already he sees himself at the head of a long caravan taking him away from the desert of the sea, toward oases of fresh water in the palm trees' jagged shade, toward palaces of thick, whitewashed walls, tiled courts where girls are dancing barefoot, moving their arms, half-hidden by their veils, and half-revealed.*[49]

Conversely, those who view the city from afar, from the desert, see Despina as a ship:

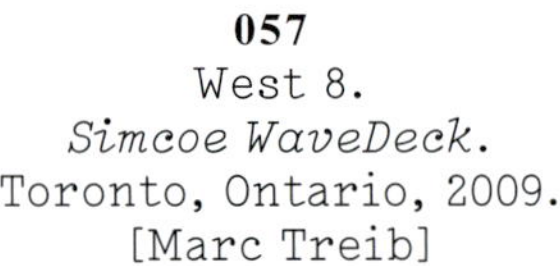

057
West 8.
Simcoe WaveDeck.
Toronto, Ontario, 2009.
[Marc Treib]

When the camel driver sees, at the horizon of the tableland, the pinnacles of the skyscrapers come into view, the radar antennae, the white and red windsocks flapping, the chimneys belching smoke, he thinks of a ship; he knows it is a city, but he thinks of it as a vessel that will take him away from the desert, a windjammer about to cast off, with the breeze already swelling the sails, not yet unfurled, or a steamboat with its boiler vibrating in the iron keel; and he thinks of all the ports, the foreign merchandise the cranes unload on the docks, the taverns where crews of different flags break bottles over one another's heads, the lighted, ground-floor windows, each with a woman combing her hair.[50]

In all, perception is a question of stance, perspective, and state of mind—and behind every major change in use is a visionary idea.

In the early years of the millennium, the Toronto shoreline underwent a substantial renovation and transformation. Propelling this radical makeover was the intention to reestablish the link between the city and Lake Ontario, converting to accessible green space land with prior uses for docking, shipping and storage. As a part of this major municipal program, in 2009 the Dutch firm West 8 energized the waterfront with a series of undulating red *WaveDecks* that broadened the shoreline pedestrian promenade, increased waterfront access, added an element of whimsy, and in places physically challenged its visitors [**057**]. The cellist Yo-Yo Ma and landscape architect Julie Messervy collaborated on another park based, so they say, on Bach's *First Suite for Unaccompanied Cello*, although the source is hardly discernable in the vegetation and topography of the pleasant landscape that resulted. Cormier's own contribution to this first phase, designed in collaboration with landscape architect Janet Rosenberg, was the HtO Park on the lakefront to the west of the city center.

H_2O + Toronto = HtO Park

From the street, the green space that today faces Queens Quay West appears to be of a normal landscape mode, although enacted in a form that became a familiar motif in Cormier's vocabulary thereafter: a huddle of "cells" perhaps best described as a spiderweb of pathways winding around the grassed mound planted with silver maples and weeping willows (*Salix babylonica*). These earth forms and clusters of trees also define the spaces of passage between them and those that lead to the lakefront [**058**] [**059**]. As a totality the elements comprise a landscape that contrasts markedly with the rigid geometry of the typical city block and erects a bulwark against the neighboring apartment blocks and the elevated Gardiner Expressway that passes not far away. More unexpectedly, in the park's southern zone, the greenery of the planted hillocks gives way to a paved walkway, a linear expanse of sand, and thereafter a wooden boardwalk that traces the edge of the shore. This "beach" zone was among Cormier's principal contributions to the project, a softening of the land's edge as it meets the water; admittedly, however, a seawall sustains the level of the beach at a meter or so above the surface of the lake [**060**].

An inspiration for the design was the series of temporary beaches—the *Paris-Plages*—installed along the River Seine each summer. A second was Georges Seurat's monumental painting *Un dimanche après-midi à l'Île de la Grande Jatte* (A Sunday

48 In 2017 Cormier proposed a "beach" and umbrellas extending along the Lake Michigan coastline in Chicago, Illinois. Due to restrictions on coastline construction, the project will not be realized.

49 Italo Calvino, *Invisible Cities*, trans. William Weaver, New York: Harcourt Brace Jovanovich, 1974, p. 17.

50 Ibid.

058
(opposite)
Claude Cormier
et Associés
with Janet Rosenberg
and Associates.
HtO Park.
Toronto, Ontario, 2007.
Aerial view.
[Janet Rosenberg Studio]

059
Claude Cormier
et Associés
with Janet Rosenberg
and Associates.
HtO Park.
View through the mounds.
[Guillaume Paradis, Claude
Cormier et Associés]

060
Claude Cormier
et Associés with Janet
Rosenberg and Associates.
HtO Park.
Toronto, Ontario, 2007.
The beach and umbrellas.
[Neil Fox]

061
Georges Seurat.
A Sunday on La Grande Jatte, 1884.
[Art Institute of Chicago, Wikimedia Commons]

on La Grande Jatte) painted in 1884, and today in the collection of the Art Institute of Chicago [061]. In the painting, the bathers look outward to the river while turning their backs on the city, just as they would in Toronto when enjoying the new park. More unusual, perhaps, were the large, yellow sheet-metal umbrellas that peppered both the sand "beach" and their adjacent walkway. The irregular placement of these shading structures foiled the relentless linearity of the beach and the accompanying walkways. The umbrellas thus served two purposes: providing shade, of course, but also anchoring the formal and spatial composition of the landscape at the water's edge. Although at far reduced scale, the effect produced by the umbrellas of the HtO beach is not unlike those of Christo and Jeanne-Claude's *The Umbrellas (Joint Project for Japan and USA)*, installed in Southern California for eighteen days in 1991 [062].[51] Unlike *The Umbrellas*, which was conceived as a temporary work of land art, however, the materials used in Toronto were made to last. The third purpose for the beachfront umbrellas was to create delight, a delight achieved by recasting a stereotypical beach item—the cloth umbrella—as an architectonic structure. In some ways the HtO Park served as the test case for the other Cormier beach projects that followed. The element of the umbrella, for example, was retained in all the subsequent beach landscapes, although the schemes for their distribution became more sophisticated in the later applications, as did the use of materials and modeling of the land surfaces.

Sugar Beach

HtO Park might be regarded as a study or prototype for the "beaches" that followed; from this first iteration, the office learned about the challenges presented by the remnants of industry on lakefront sites, human behavior, the performance of materials when confronting a challenging environment, and even the composition of the sand used to carpet the park's primary surfaces. The experience and knowledge acquired would be first applied to the design of Sugar Beach, a project on a site east of Toronto's center, in the East Bayfront neighborhood being developed in the early part of the new millennium. The commission resulted from an international invited design competition with a requirement for the submission of a preliminary design. The Cormier idea for the park was simple yet original: to convert a parking lot into a beach. Again, a painting by Georges Seurat provided the generating

51 In parallel with the giant yellow umbrellas that composed the Californian half of the art project, there were over a thousand sky-blue umbrellas installed in Ibaraki, Japan, during the same period.

structure: *Une Baignade, Asnières (*known in English as *Bathers at Asnières*), in which an idyllic riverbank is set against a background filled with gritty structures and the smoke of industry. Analogous to the content of the painting, Sugar Beach would offer a respite from the industrial milieu in which it was situated. Sand would be the principal "paving" material and sand would cover most of the site. Greenery would be added only where needed, and a digitally activated field of water jets would induce screams and giggles from children, and offer them—and the adults who might also dare—water play denied by the lack of physical contact with the lake itself.

062
Christo and Jeanne-Claude. *The Umbrellas, Japan-USA*, 1984-1991. © Christo Tejon Pass, California. [Marc Treib]

The site of the new Sugar Beach, formerly a parking area serving local industry, had been declared a segment of the lakefront zone then in the process of being converted to arts facilities, housing, and recreational uses [**063**] [**064**]. Facing the site was the massive brick home of the Redpath Sugar Refinery—its function would lend the park its name—whose great bulk is augmented periodically by the arrival of ships of major dimensions and volumes into the slip that separates the refinery from the Sugar Beach site. At times of unloading, the air is filled with a mist of sugar that is almost palpable. The relationship of park to water is simple: look, but don't touch. The master plan by West 8 and DTAH routed foot traffic along the lake, literally following the outer edge of the park site. The first, and perhaps most consequential, aspect of the Cormier proposal was to reroute the pedestrian path away from the water and join it to the lakefront promenade as a diagonal path. By so doing, the park site was rendered a wedge removed from the intrusions of major pedestrian circulation. The routing also assured visitors a direct visual connection with the water, the refinery, and periodically, passing and berthed ships.

The diagonal walkway that edges the site shares the same width as the corresponding segments of the lakefront promenade; weeping willows, Jefferson maples (*Acer freemanii*), and white pines (*Pinus strobus*) define its edge and shield the beach proper from the passing crowds [**065**] [**066**] [**067**]. Employing the same maple-leaf paving motif designed by West 8 and DTAH, and executed in two shades of gray granite, the promenade is quietly ornamental; the maple-leaf paving also shapes the field of water jets in the children's play area [**068**]. To bolster the separation of the two primary zones—beach and promenade—and to give dimension to the landscape, the landscape architects installed two gigantic granite boulders quarried in the Canadian Shield and brought to Toronto in pieces and assembled on-site

063
(previous page)
Sugar Beach.
Toronto, Ontario, 2010.
Aerial view showing
diagonal promenade,
shortly after completion.
[Vito Riccio]

064
Sugar Beach.
Aerial view showing
tree growth along
the promenade; photo
taken in 2017.
[Industryous Photography]

065
(previous page)
Sugar Beach.
The promenade in 2014 with the lake view.
[Guillaume Paradis, Claude Cormier et Associés]

066
Sugar Beach.
Toronto, Ontario, 2010.
Looking through the willows, across the beach, to the boat slip beyond.
[Marc Treib]

067
Sugar Beach.
Toronto, Ontario, 2010.
Sugar Beach willows with ship and refinery behind.
[Industryous Photography]

068
Sugar Beach.
Maple leaf-shaped platform animated by water jets.
[Claude Cormier et Associés]

069
(opposite)
Sugar Beach.
The boulder as bicycle challenge.
[Jesse Colin Jackson]

070
Sugar Beach.
Toronto, Ontario, 2010.
The boulder as seat.
[Marc Treib]

071
Sugar Beach.
Children playing among
the water jets.
[Nicola Betts]

072
Sugar Beach.
The Beach.
[Nicola Betts]

thereafter [069] [070]. Red and white lines executed in thermoplastic trace the joints of the assembled boulders and mark their contours—they also suggest the stripes on hard rock candy in particular, and sugar more generally. The grid of water jets, programmed by computer to dance and play, marks the lakeside entrance to the beach and delights the children who may be frustrated by their forced remove from the expanse of water flowing before their eyes [071]. Those are the elements of the design. Oh, but yes, there are also those pink umbrellas.

The commissioning authorities were not thrilled with the nomination of pink as the color of the umbrellas and requested that another hue might be more suitable. In a reaction typical for the office, Cormier and company fought head-on the directive of the review board—as they would when later proposing the dog fountain at Berczy Park—with a visual presentation of the color pink that culminated with a photo of Jacqueline Kennedy wearing a chic pink outfit with matching pillbox hat. Once again, the authorities relented. The pink of the umbrellas, in fact, adds a welcome degree of levity to an otherwise somber industrial site, especially when aided by the field of white sand [072]. Sugar Beach uses a special mix formulated to correct the shortcomings of the sand used in the HtO Park some years before. Along the water, a boardwalk suggests a leisurely stroll removed from the sand for those who come only to walk and view. The size of the umbrellas was also called into question: would they be large enough to shelter, for example, an entire family? With tongue in cheek the Cormier office's Christmas card that year depicted the Holy Family-cum-Magi, all sheltered comfortably beneath a pink umbrella far from a manger in Bethlehem. Yes, the umbrellas would be of sufficient size. Individual chairs rather than benches lend a personal scale to the site; their position may be shifted slightly, but they cannot be moved freely.

It is so easy to get wrapped up in the imagery, playfulness, and whimsy of projects such as these that we may overlook or forget the devotion to technical issues that lies behind them. Designs by the Cormier office are always well resolved and carefully detailed. They are made to last; an image means nothing if its existence is only transitory, unless of course that is the specific nature of the design task, as for an art installation. The fiberglass umbrellas, by the industrial designer Andrew Jones, were made to withstand high winds and vandalism, and included lighting built into their peaks for nighttime use.[52] The experience with the umbrellas at the HtO Park taught the design team how to better detail the segments that comprise the umbrellas and determine their arrangement on the beach. Given the absence of ground covers and lawn areas, and the limited number of trees set only on the periphery, the need for constant maintenance has been minimized. Although the technology for the dancing water jets that mark the entrance to the beach near the lake has been used for decades, there were still issues controlling the flow through the nozzles and the height and duration of the emissions. In addition, displacing, hauling, and installing substantial amounts of granite is no easy matter; every aspect of the rocks' excavation in the Canadian Shield was clearly specified and carefully directed, as was their installation on the Sugar Beach site. The country singer Dolly Parton once famously said, "It costs a lot of money to look this cheap." In a similar way, it takes a lot of study and effort to produce a work that looks "dumb" and "natural," so that it appears to have been made without effort or much thought. Appearances can be deceiving.

52 As it happens, this proved not to be a good idea as the lamps raised technical difficulties.

Clock Tower Beach

The third in the series of surrogate beaches was constructed in the Vieux-Port de Montréal, and resulted almost entirely from a product of Cormier's imagination and initiative. The assignment originally given the office was to provide for parking on a narrow and tapering peninsula, in actuality a quay of substantial mass, set between the bassin de l'Horloge and the Saint Lawrence River. This area was intended to accommodate the cars driven by visitors to the historic Clock Tower and the section of the Old Town that fronts the river [073]. The commission at first seemed to be straightforward and pragmatic although Cormier was given some latitude to propose solutions more creative than simply providing 400 parking spaces or accommodating the turning radii of cars. Paving such a significant area of the site, with its consequent impermeability, would have demanded engineered drainage to manage the volume of rain and snow that falls annually. The project's engineers determined that a culvert of an impressive cross section would be required to collect, manage, and disperse the predicted amount of drainage. Instead, Cormier reasoned, by sloping the paving into two large permeable bioswales, the diameter of the pipe could be dramatically reduced, or even eliminated, thus saving a sum of money that ran into the millions of dollars. With these savings the landscape architect proposed a beach that would convert the land at the point of the jetty into a recreational space to be enjoyed by all.

Greeting visitors are structures converted from shipping containers, designed by Birtz Bastien Beaudoin Laforest, that house ticketing, washrooms, and a small café. Made of steel for economy, the structures are painted a vibrant sky blue like the umbrellas for which they serve as entry and support. Unlike Sugar Beach, Clock Tower Beach is set roughly eleven feet (three meters) below street level, almost at the level of the river. While on the one hand, this allowed the new beach to approach the actual surface of the water, it also required some device to bring visitors from the parking area to the sand. The solution was a broad flight of concrete stairs that led in two directions set perpendicular to one another [074]. One flight leads to the main beach at the point, the second to the boat slip between the quai de l'Horloge and the Old Town. To accommodate universal accessibility a ramp is inscribed within the stairs, following the "stramp" prototype pioneered by Cornelia Hahn Oberlander in her 1970s landscape design for Robson Square in Vancouver.[53]

Applying the lessons learned at HtO Park and Sugar Beach, at Clock Tower Beach, Cormier again adjusted the sand mixture, to one lighter in color and softer in texture. The umbrellas have been further refined and painted two shades of blue that display an affinity to a clear sky or shallow water while recalling the *Blue Tree* at Cornerstone [075]. Because an admission fee is charged and entry controlled, the chairs on the beach could be freely movable. This flexibility, which was not possible at the two earlier editions of the beach due to their open access, allows new configurations of chairs to accommodate social groups and facilitates easy adjustments to attract or deter the sun. A wooden boardwalk at the base of the retaining wall in the bassin de l'Horloge has been planted with Boston ivy, converting it into a long green wall that softens its presence [076] [077]. The corresponding wall that faces it on the opposite side of the basin has been similarly treated. In all, although Sugar Beach is probably the best known and most used of Cormier's waterfront projects, this third iteration in Montréal in some ways represents the perfection of the idea on formal terms.

53 These were nicknamed "stramps"—a conflation of stairs and ramps.

073
Clock Tower Beach.
Old Port, Montréal,
Québec, 2012.
Aerial view showing
beach, parking,
and boat basin.
[Guillaume Paradis, Claude
Cormier et Associés]

074
Clock Tower Beach.
Old Port, Montréal,
Québec, 2012.
The “stramps” connecting
the parking level with
the beach.
[Marc Treib]

075
Clock Tower Beach.
Old Port, Montréal,
Québec, 2012.
The beach at the point.
[Raphaël Thibodeau]

076
Clock Tower Beach.
Old Port, Montréal,
Québec, 2012.
Ivy, visible along
the wooden deck,
covers retaining walls
in the boat basin.
[Raphael Thibodeau]

077
Clock Tower Beach.
The beach in winter.
[Claude Cormier
et Associés]

Of the two remaining beaches, only one has been or will be constructed. The project for the AIDS memorial beach along Lake Michigan in Chicago was terminated due to the restrictions imposed on any new shoreline construction. In the design for the memorial Cormier had returned, once again, to brightly colored metal umbrellas, seemingly scattered along and across the stone steps of the breakwater.[54] Such an intervention contradicted the requirement to keep the breakwaters free of additional elements, however, and in response, the proposal was withdrawn.

Completed in summer 2018, Breakwater Park in Kingston, Ontario, is sophisticated in its address of complex environmental and social issues, and marked by enhanced amenity, if offering less than the usual amount of Cormier levity. And unlike the earlier waterside projects, Breakwater Park actually brings people to the water and assists their entry. This site is unusual, located just where the Saint Lawrence River meets Lake Ontario. The campus of the elite Queen's University lies just north of the park, which has already become a favorite destination for the students. Nearby are the Tett Centre for Creativity and Learning and the Queen's University Isabel Bader Performing Arts Centre [078] [079]. A still-functioning water purification plant anchors the site's western edge, and beyond it stands a jail. At the purification plant a pier long removed from service in earlier days provided a landing to the water treatment plant from the lake. In prior years the shoreline had been heavily engineered to counter the effects of major storms and destructive swells, bolstering the fight against erosion with massive rockwork. While a shoreline promenade existed, there was no beach: entering the water was a challenge, and in fact, swimming along this segment of the shore was illegal. Nonetheless, swimming had become common practice.

The program called for a renovation of the existing facilities including increased —now legal—public entry to the lake. Cormier extended the requirements of the brief by providing intermittent water access along the full length of the shoreline, in places with ramps, in others with steps. While the eastern segment is primarily devoted to the promenade, the western end includes large stone slabs used for sunbathing and a beach area that in good weather is filled with people, many of them Queen's University students equally interested, it seems, in taking the sun, perhaps swimming, and displaying their bodies.

The idea behind the design—which conceptually divides into two primary zones—is to restore, replace, and add—all accomplished using features that are almost always understated. The lakefront promenade, for example, reworks an existing allée of silver maples (*Acer saccharinum*) into a strong link that connects the eastern and western zones; every effort was made to utilize the volume and beauty of the trees and to protect them during construction. New trees were planted as needed. The simple concrete walkway widened or replaced the existing path, with the soil from excavation needed for any subsurface stabilization used to model a series of soft mounds in the green part of the park along King Street. The linear terraces of concrete that protect the shoreline against the adverse force of storms double as staged bleachers for sitting, picnicking, stretching out, or sunbathing [080]. In all, the eastern zone is essentially devoted to passive recreation and circulation, including a gravel-covered concrete ramp to facilitate universal access to the lake. In contrast, the western zone offers more sites for active recreation. An expansive lawn, set in parallel to the beach area on the opposite of the path, is the

54 Cormier believed that selling individual umbrellas would have raised sufficient funding to cover the cost of construction.

078
Breakwater Park.
Kingston, Ontario, 2018.
Aerial view showing relation to Queen's University and the urban fabric of Kingston.
[Industryous Photography]

079
(overleaf)
Breakwater Park.
Aerial view showing pier, bridge, and sheltered cove with universal access.
[Industryous Photography]

“hinge” that joins land and water. As it was originally dedicated to a kind of kite-surfing, the program mandated that this area must be free of trees and other potential obstacles —like the signature Cormier umbrellas. At the water end of the narrow panel of sand beach, a flight of staged terraces eases access to the lake. One end of the old pier has become a platform from which to dive while the other offers a flat plane of concrete, sheltered in part by a pergola for partial protection from the sun. Although it was possible to get to the pier using the existing structure, the route was circuitous. To make access more direct, the Cormier team proposed a new footbridge to cross over the cove [081]. Originally projected to be built of shiny stainless steel to reflect the water below it, the bridge—still of the office's design—was built with more ordinary steel construction, which may actually be more appropriate.

Unlike the prior Cormier “beaches,” here slabs of stone along the promenade form a linear set of steps that facilitates entry to the water [082]. Thoughtful consideration has been devoted to universal access. Along the promenade, for example, the slabs beneath the seating and picnic tables have been widened to accommodate wheelchairs, with a small curb added to prevent unintended entry into the lawn areas. The most unusual and engaging feature of the proposal was the conversion of the cove into a protected area for wading and swimming. Near the point of access, the cove has been lined with a concrete slab and covered with pebbles. A ramp provides access for children, the infirm, and those wheelchair-bound. This feature represents the considerate thought that lies behind the forms and the care with which the office undertakes its designs.

Dedicated to the late Gord Downie, frontman of the Kingston-based rock band The Tragically Hip, the new Breakwater Park skillfully reworked existing facilities along the shore and integrated them with new features to expand the appeal and uses of a venue already popular with multiple segments of the population—from windsurfers to dog walkers. Although completed only several months ago, the park's identity as a destination and enormous popularity has caused some disgruntled citizens to call for restrictions on its open hours.[55] In designing and realizing the park Claude Cormier et Associés were serious about design; it's the people in Kingston who get to have the fun [083].

Like Frederick Law Olmsted, Sr., one might look at the institution of the park as the injection of the country into the city, *rus in urbe*, required by an urban population. With a modern twist, the series of urban beaches in Toronto and Montréal represent a contemporary and innovative recollection of that tradition, bringing to those unable to leave the city, or those who choose not to, certain amenities provided by the rural countryside, or in this particular case, the shore. On the one hand, one might interpret the beach projects as deception: although they evoke the image of a beach, they offer only the visual, auditory, and at times olfactory experience of water and shore without true physical access to the river or lake. As such they offer the look but not the reality. Oscar Wilde once quipped, “To be natural is such a very difficult pose to keep up”; Cormier makes no such effort to be natural and might agree that landscape architecture itself is an unnatural act.[56] But here we best consider these beaches as a simile or borderline metaphor, landscapes that provide only some selected amenities afforded by a true beach, an evocation, a simulacrum of the seaside experience. Admittedly, most of them do not provide all the benefits of a real beach, but they certainly meet their users more

55 https://globalnews.ca/news/4646506/kingston-resident-proposes-curfew-gordon-edgar-downie-pier/.

56 Oscar Wilde, *An Ideal Husband*, quoted in Sontag, “Notes on ‘Camp,’” p. 282.

080
Breakwater Park.
Kingston, Ontario, 2018.
The shoreline promenade.
[Industryous Photography]

081
Breakwater Park.
The bridge with
pier beyond.
[Industryous Photography]

082
Breakwater Park.
Rock slabs along
the shoreline.
[Industryous Photography]

083
(overleaf)
Breakwater Park.
Fun on (and from)
the bridge.
[Industryous Photography]

GORD EDGAR DOWNIE PIER

084
Breakwater Park.
Kingston, Ontario, 2018.
The beach supports both
active and passive uses.
[Industryous Photography]

085
Breakwater Park.
Staged levels ease access
to the water.
[Marc Treib]

086
Christopher Tunnard; Gordon Cullen, delineator. "Plants with grey foliage." [*Gardens in the Modern Landscape*, 1938; drawing © Gordon Cullen Estate.]

than halfway. Their success has been verified by the throngs of people who use these parks in all kinds of weather and who seem little troubled that access to the water is not possible—and revel in it at Breakwater Park, when it is. For those who remain on the shore, the sand, umbrellas, and chairs are enough, perhaps more than enough, to draw them to the place and to enjoy their time spent there [**084**]. When swimming is facilitated, the gift is even greater [**085**].

The Position of Plants

Given the emphasis to this point on the imagery that characterizes many a Cormier landscape, one might deduce that in their making plants have played only a limited role. To some degree, this is an accurate assessment. Unlike the garden designer whose plans may derive from the favored prominence of even a single species—or as we have seen in reference to Gertrude Jekyll, the mixture of species to achieve maximum chromatic effect—in most Cormier landscapes, plants may play a subsidiary role—although often a consequential one. The use of plants for what they do, rather than for just how they look or smell, positions Cormier in the modernist tradition. In the first half of the twentieth century, landscape architects such as Christopher Tunnard rejected the use of plants solely for the their attractiveness or rarity, and argued instead for what Tunnard termed a "structural" use of vegetation [**086**].[57] The true value of the plant was less its appearance or rarity than its ability to define and structure space. Tunnard was joined by Garrett Eckbo in his 1950 manifesto *Landscape for Living* in which Eckbo stated, "Structure is thought of as THE art of spatial design, but planting is likewise an art of spatial design—the primary spatial control out-of-doors, equal qualitatively to structural design though varying in kind [**087**]."[58] Countering the universality of such assertions is the obvious fact that many plants are regarded as interesting and even beautiful for their color and form, and perhaps of greater significance, for their power to create a biologically dynamic and visually charged landscape that changes throughout the cycles of the year. That notion of change—to which must be added growth over the years—is a prominent characteristic of landscape architecture, and one of the factors that distinguishes the discipline from traditional notions of sculpture.

57 Christopher Tunnard, *Gardens in the Modern Landscape*, London: Architectural Press, 1938.

58 Garrett Eckbo, *Landscape for Living*, New York: Duell, Sloan and Pearce, 1950, p. 95. However, Eckbo was not categorical, writing that plant selection "must be worked out in terms of *selection*, *arrangement*, and *maintenance*" (italics in the original). Ibid., p. 96.

In response to my question about his selection and use of plants, Cormier responded jokingly that since Montréal and Toronto occupy territory listed in Canadian Hardiness Zone 6, there are only a very limited number of trees from which to choose—that is, should the plants be restricted to native species.[59] Principal among these are maples (*Acer saccharinum*, *Acer rubrum*, *Acer x freemanii*), elm (*Ulmus americana* and hybrids), spruce (*Picea glauca*), linden (*Tilia*), hackberry (*Celtis*), and honey locust (*Gleditsia*). While it is true that plants tend to play a supporting role in many Cormier landscapes, that generalization does not apply to all of them. For example, the 2002 Esplanade that accompanied the Montréal Palais des congrès was configured as a set of low, almost elliptical, mounds that filled a zone roughly ovular in shape—earthen mounds set on the concrete slab that roofed the parking garage below [**088**]. These urban hillocks were configured to provide sufficient soil for the grove of crab apple trees (*Malus* 'Makamik') that would be the Esplanade's dominant feature. The mounds were planted with spirea to stabilize the earth and gently nudge visitors to keep to the benches placed along the paths that wound through the earth forms and shrubbery. The crab apple grove rises from the mounds and provides welcome shade during the hot, humid months of summer, dappled sunlight in autumn, and of course, a brilliant flash of pink blooms in early spring [**089**]. Obviously, neither conifer nor nonflowering tree nor low shrub would have contributed as much to the quality and interest of the landscape and the comfort it provides visitors. The selection of species was apt.

The 2010 courtyard adjacent to the Hydro-Québec office tower in Montréal serves as a pass-through and entrance court as well as a pocket park for locals [**090**]. The design of the plaza/park accompanied the renovation of the offices for the province's Maison du développement durable (Agency for Sustainable Development) that borders the court on its southwest side. In contrast to those Cormier landscapes in which hard, durable, or even synthetic materials prevail, here a mix of indigenous woodland plants and trees plays the lead role in propagating a small urban drama.[60] To support the survival of woodland plants in the city, and for maximum protection from intrusion, whether

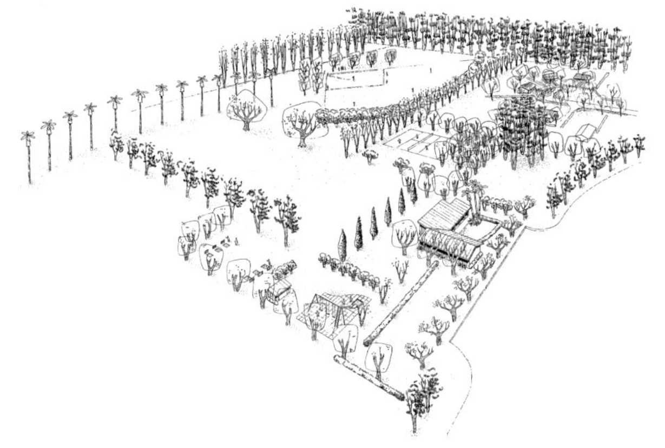

087
Garrett Eckbo.
Community park.
Central Valley, California,
late 1930s.
Trees used to define space.
[Marc Treib Collection]

59 Claude Cormier, in conversation, Montréal, July 2017.

60 The Maison du développement durable required an "all-indigenous planting palette." It often happens that "indigenous plants in the north need very specific conditions to thrive and might not be as hardy as other horticultural varieties—letting the opportunists conquer all of the real estate." Georges-Étienne Parent, email to Marc Treib, 14 June 2018.

088
Esplanade du Palais
des congrès de Montréal.
Montréal, Québec, 2002.
View from above soon
after planting.
[Jean-François Vézina]

089
(overleaf)
Esplanade du Palais
des congrès de Montréal.
The crab apples in bloom.
[Guillaume Paradis, Claude
Cormier et Associés]

090
(opposite)
Parc Hydro-Québec.
Montréal, Québec, 2012.
Site plan.
[Claude Cormier
et Associés]

091
Parc Hydro-Québec.
Walkway surfaces
of galvanized steel under
a honey locust canopy.
[Claude Cormier
et Associés]

092
Parc Hydro-Québec.
Planting detail.
[Marc Treib]

human or animal, the "floor" of the plaza was set some one-and-a-half feet (some forty-five centimeters) above the ground, with mixed woodland planting beneath it extending wall to wall [091] [092]. The walkways were constructed of galvanized steel mesh to support pedestrian circulation while allowing rain to permeate and nourish the vegetation below. Adjacent to the buildings, the metal walkway—which in plan has been given a geometric shape said to recall electrical power towers—was withheld from the façades to create voids that encourage the growth of plants of greater size. The trees that rise above the metal "floor" and roof the space are honey locust (*Gleditsia triacanthos*), a deciduous species with pinnate leaves, whose canopy effectively filters sunlight and projects it onto the court's surface as a delicate pattern of light and shadow. In autumn, the leaves turn a brilliant yellow that animates the small grove and the quarter around it. Despite trying urban conditions, the trees have done well and have been the key "structural" element of the vegetation plan. All did not proceed completely as planned and hoped, however, as limited maintenance has once again hampered the survival and growth of the vegetation. Below the tree canopies, the ground was originally planted with a mix of ground covers and low plants, but over time most of these have disappeared; however, some plants, such as Christmas fern (*Polystichum acrostichoides*) and bush honeysuckle (*Diervilla lonicera*) continue to prosper.

Of any project undertaken in the twenty-five years of Claude Cormier et Associés, the landscape for the Evergreen Brick Works relied the most heavily on vegetation and used the most extensive number of species —despite the project's being primarily a conversion from industrial to educational use [093]. The site of today's Evergreen complex, set on the eastern edge of Toronto, first hosted a paper mill constructed in the opening decades of the nineteenth century. When excellent clay for making bricks was discovered, however, on-site production was converted to the manufacture of bricks.[61] Opened in 1889, the Don Valley Brick Works maintained a thriving business for almost a century; brick production continued under various ownerships into the 1980s, at which time the clay reserves on-site had become exhausted. New uses for the land as a park and educational center began in the early 1990s, at which time landscape architect Michael Hough created a series of trails through second-growth vegetation, indigenous and exotic, restored indigenous species, and converted the former quarry into a pond fronting the industrial buildings once dedicated to shaping and firing bricks. In 2006 an international Request for Qualifications was issued; the commission was awarded to a multidisciplinary team that included DTAH, ERA Architects, Diamond Schmitt, and Claude Cormier et Associés. At that time, about a decade after the center's initial opening in 1991, the Cormier office continued the initial landscape efforts by designing the parking, entry, and office areas for the current owner, Evergreen, a nonprofit foundation that envisioned the brick works landscape as "a demonstration hub where the world can experience sustainable practices that enable flourishing cities of the future."[62] The center is today known as Evergreen Brick Works.[63]

Occupying land at the base of a ravine, the forces acting on the Evergreen site are hardly benign. Drainage is a major issue as the land, situated in a floodplain, is subject to inundation during periods of heavy rain or snowmelt. In all, because the land is dynamic, any appropriate scheme must mitigate the passage of potentially hostile natural forces flowing both through and across the site. The design concept hinged on the notion of a "village" rather than a complex of industrial buildings per se, an understandable direction given the mixed uses the project was to serve. To Cormier, the design needed to address the tripartite program of "children, education, and nature," but most of all he believed that the new Evergreen Brick Works had to preserve the "magic" already existing on-site.[64] Functionally, the scheme needed to facilitate easy access, provide adequate parking, and accommodate weekend farmers markets, environmental education programs, play—and ice skating. Those were only the programmatic needs, however.

Although the paved parking areas are straightforward, sparsely planted, and undistinguished, new plantings in circular raised planters buffer the zone between the parking areas and the industrial structures that today compose the educational and ecological center from the main road. Reprising a motif used in prior projects such as the Esplanade for the Palais des congrès, the series of large circular planters that form the Tiffany Commons have been filled with dense plantings of varying species [094]. The most prominent of the planters supports a small grove of birches; in others, native species of lower heights prevail. The low concrete retaining walls that surround the perimeters of the planters have been set at a height appropriate for seating. A heroically scaled pergola inundated with wild grapevines serves as the formal entry to the complex almost in the manner of a *propylaea*, an especially effective greeting for those arriving by shuttle bus on weekdays [095].[65] The vegetation surrounding each of the surviving buildings displays a rich mixture of native woodland plants such as sumac, poplar, willow, and milkweed that together produce an intricate chromatic interplay of greens and leaf textures [096]. To the untrained eye, these pools of greenery may appear as spontaneous natural growth, although, in fact, all the vegetation has been carefully studied, selected, installed, and calculated to prosper under the conditions imposed by the new uses.

The most dramatic transformation of the prior industrial works was the removal of the roof of the former brickmaking facility, converting it to use as a space for school outings, social events, and corporate meetings: the Koerner Gardens [097]. The circular planters that populate the Tiffany Commons in the entrance area reappear within the historical brick walls of the factory as a consistent design element that conjoins the areas of the design scheme and produces a sense of continuity. Dense plantings of shrubs and trees, many of them selected and planted by the center's personnel, fill the circular beds set within the rectangular confines of the old building. Stands of pines such as Eastern white pine (*Pinus strobus*) and spruces—now grown to sizeable dimensions—conjure an impression of the Canadian woods until a fragment of the brick walls standing behind the vegetation comes into view and confounds that first image. The rehearsal of design elements, paired with the naturalistic plantings, convincingly conflates indoors and out; the venerable brick walls of the original factory provide the frame. Unroofed and open to the sky, the space spans nature and culture, history and the present. The most dramatic transformation of the Koerner Gardens occurs each winter when controlled flooding—contained within

61 https://en.wikipedia.org/wiki/Don_Valley_Brick_Works This site is also the source of subsequent historical data cited here.

62 https://www.evergreen.ca/evergreen-brick-works/.

63 Other buildings have been converted to use by nonprofits such as the Centre for Green Cities. "Design and construction was a joint venture between Du Toit Allsopp Hiller Architects [DTAH], Diamond Schmitt Architects, and several other prominent firms. DTAH is responsible for the master planning scheme, while Diamond Schmitt are the designers of the new Centre for Green Cities and Welcome Centre." https://en.wikipedia.org/wiki/Don_Valley_Brick_Works.

64 Cormier, "Serious Fun," lecture.

65 Due to the larger number of cars on weekend, the drop-off point is shifted to a location near the main road.

EVERGREEN
BRICK WORKS
www.evergreen.ca

093
Evergreen Brick Works.
Toronto, Ontario, 2010.
The complex from above.
[Industryous Photography]

094
(overleaf)
Evergreen Brick Works.
Entrance area with
raised planters.
[Industryous Photography]

Nature at Work

WELCOME

095
(opposite)
Evergreen Brick Works.
Toronto, Ontario, 2010.
Tiffany Foundation Urban
Grape Trellis, 2013.
[Industryous Photography]

096
Evergreen Brick Works.
Campus landscape
with native plants.
[Industryous Photography]

097
Evergreen Brick Works. Toronto, Ontario, 2010. The Koerner Gardens within the old walls of the factory. [Claude Cormier et Associés]

098
Evergreen Brick Works. The Koerner Gardens used for ice skating in winter. [Bryce Miranda]

the low concrete curbs that bound the planting areas—becomes frozen, and the whole space, as if by magic, is turned to ice for new uses such as skating [098].

To restate: Although in many Cormier projects vegetation plays a subsidiary role, several of the office's projects demonstrate that when appropriate, plants and trees have been critical for the conception and realization of the design. In these works, Cormier returns to lessons learned from his early studies in agronomy, while profiting as well from his three decades of experience in urban and suburban planting design. In his work the role of the plants can be significant in the success of the project.

Adding Value

In lectures and in conversation, Cormier has frequently stressed that as a landscape architect he sees one of his roles is to "add value" to the project, i.e., not only to the client's investment, but also to the public good. In several landscapes for developers the value has appeared as a more attractive frontispiece for the building(s) that adds positively to the city's greenery while invoking an affirmative first impression. These concerns represent value not solely in terms of amplified return on investment but also as value added to the cityscape and public realm. Such gestures can be especially prized in the northern latitudes where the winter is long and the skies are often overcast and gray. Value is also found in the landscape architect's mining of the program to discover what more can be accrued within the limits of the budget. As discussed above, while working on a parking area in the Old Port of Montréal, Cormier realized that by creating a bioswale between the ranks of parking, the need for a major drainage pipe could be virtually eliminated. The money saved by this modification to the site engineering funded the making of the third Cormier "beach," an amenity much appreciated by the citizens. Added value.

The entrance plaza for the 57-floor Four Seasons Hotel and Towers was conceived as an overscaled Victorian carpet, a welcome mat for guests arriving at the hotel and a silent farewell for those who depart [099]. A supersized cast-aluminum fountain in the style of Berczy Park occupies the center of the site.[66] By carefully calculating the surface area needed for arrival, pickups, and parking, and after extensive discussions with the clients, Cormier was able to assign the remaining segment of the site to a small green park: privately owned by the hotel and the condominium, but with free access given the public [100] [101]. As a result, Toronto received a new public space as "added value." The rose served as the motif and point of departure for the design of the park, and like the pattern of petals swirling outward from the flower's center, the landscape developed in layers of roughly concentric, stepped levels edged with limestone planks. Cormier terms the landscape "a rose garden without roses."[67] A grove of honey locusts "roofs" the retreat, and movable chairs provide comfort on what topographically is a gently modeled earthen mound. A rear wall of stainless steel created by artist Linda Covit and laser cut with a line drawing of a rose backdrops the new park, while misters periodically add a touch of cool and sense of mystery to the greenery. While it must be admitted that certain of the details here are not as sophisticated as in other Cormier landscapes, and in places the resolution of geometry in regard to visitor movement is less than perfect, the net result is nevertheless a pocket park offering its visitors a reprieve from the nearly continuous and noisy

66 Cormier notes that due to the hotel's concern about wind, the fountain is rarely turned on—today it's "more of a bird bath." In conversation, Montréal, July 2017.

67 Cormier, lecture, Gardner Museum.

099
Four Seasons Hotel
and Residences.
Toronto, Ontario, 2012.
Paving configured as giant
Victorian urban carpet
to welcome guests.
[John Consolati]

100
(opposite)
Four Seasons Hotel
and Residences.
The park as a rose
with concentric rings
of hedges.
[Paul Casselman]

101
Four Seasons Hotel
and Residences.
Toronto, Ontario, 2012.
[Brent Raymond]

traffic that passes by [102]. In this and other works, the landscape architect saw a responsibility to the public as well to the client, whose program and demeanor, fortunately, allowed a broadening of the brief to also provide for the public good. In lectures Cormier has claimed an identity shared with Robin Hood, who according to myth took from the rich to give to the poor. While neither his persona nor his deeds have been quite as dramatic as his legendary English predecessor—and his efforts are far from actual theft—in many projects the landscape architect's contribution has rendered public terrain that might only have remained in private hands.

Added value, to Claude Cormier, constitutes more than increased savings or monetary return for the sponsoring client. Value to the public—or at the very least, to the users of a private landscape—should augment the address of the functional program. At times added value may take physical form as increased public open space or a bench in just the right place; at other times, added value may be more psychological, like a feeling of well-being, or just a smile, or even perhaps a real laugh. Regardless of the form of its realization, added value implies something beyond what is required, something given as an act of empathy, like a beach to an industrial waterfront or a seat to a weary shopper.

In Closing

In the twenty-five years of its existence Claude Cormier et Associés have achieved notable professional success and recognition for a host of innovative works, whether these qualify as landscape architecture or public art. In the international landscape community it is one of very few firms whose projects span the two practices on a regular basis; in Canada, it is unique. It is easy to smile or laugh at works like the dog fountain at Berczy Park, and perhaps even dismiss the concoction as kitsch and thus not warranting critical attention. This, I feel, would be a serious error. Keep in mind that laughter can itself be healing, not to mention the need for sites that serve as destinations for the daily dog walk that brings the elderly and others outdoors on a regular basis. Although humor may play a large role in some Cormier landscapes, as we have seen, it is hardly the only dimension or value these landscapes possess. Beneath the smile always lies amenity, and beneath the amenity lies a respect for the context, whether social, environmental, urban, or more natural. These are responsible landscapes first, and humor-inducing sites second. Yes, dogs, and cats, and flowers—and even pink umbrellas and dancing waters—can be fun, but the design thinking behind them is quite serious. Yes, at times the landscapes appear more serious, at other times more filled with mirth. Like life itself. But even when teeming with glee, this delight is always executed with a considerable dose of seriousness. In all, although it may first appear just as fun, it's always serious fun, which can be a notable accomplishment in and of itself.

102
Four Seasons Hotel
and Residences.
Toronto, Ontario, 2012.
The rear wall of
stainless steel with the
line drawings of roses
by Linda Covit.
[Marc Treib]

103
Dorchester Square,
North Portion.
Montréal, Québec, 2019.
Close-up view of
the sliced fountain.
[Jean Blais]

The Beauty of Serious Fun

Susan Herrington

Any attempt to capture the serious fun of Claude Cormier's landscape architecture may seem out of step to some people. Much landscape architectural writing today evokes ecology as its chief metaphor, and equipped with the moral certainty of networks and systems, these authors would surely have little patience for the yummy bling of Sugar Beach, the enchanting canines of Berczy Park, or the willful designer who rose from obscurity on a remote Québec farm to imagine and realize these resplendent places today. Even my coauthor, Marc Treib, asks in his chapter's introductory paragraph, "Do we really need" this? Of course, his answer is "Yes; yes, we do." I agree, and I think I know why.

We need Cormier's landscapes because they are beautiful, and many of them are leavened with humor that brings joy to the countless people who use them [**103**]. The mention of the word "beauty" may appear naïve to some critics or at least a poor word choice. During the last half of the twentieth century, beauty became increasingly devalued in the art and art-related worlds. Several decades ago, if a critic deemed an Abstract Expressionist painting beautiful, it would likely be taken as an insult. At that time, "the picture was no longer supposed to be Beautiful, but True—an accurate representation or equivalence of the artist's interior sensation and experience."[1] Conceptual artists, likewise, shunned beauty. Instead, they sought to engage viewers cognitively, "because art should be about intellectual inquiry and reflection rather than beauty and aesthetic pleasure (as traditionally conceived)."[2] Feminists, too, argued that much of the Western art world objectified women as passive objects of beauty to be enjoyed by heterosexual men, while at the same time ignoring women artists themselves. As the philosopher Alexander Nehamas surmised, "In all its forms, beauty came to seem morally and politically suspect as well as intellectually embarrassing."[3]

As attention shifted toward ecological performance—during the late 1960s and 1970s under the sway of the fiery dictums of Ian McHarg—the role of beauty in built works of landscape architecture was also derided. The emphasis on ecology today, too, often ignores the role of beauty. Elizabeth K. Meyer notes that landscape architects who are primarily concerned with performative landscapes or ecological remediation often downplay beauty. She describes how a colleague's fascination with "the performative blinded him to the distinction between beauty and beautification or ornamentation. He did not think beauty mattered, or realize that appearance could perform."[4] Meyer argues that the pursuit of beauty could help landscape architects develop an environmental ethic, noting, "a beautiful landscape works on our psyche, affording the chance to ponder on a world outside ourselves."[5]

Meyer's conception of beauty builds upon that of Elaine Scarry's. In *On Beauty and Being Just*, Scarry argues that beauty leads us not away from ethical concerns, but toward an understanding of others. Tracing the etymology of "being fair" in European, Eastern European, and Sanskrit languages, as meaning "being beautiful," she proposes that beauty is connected to fairness, meaning equal treatment. According to Scarry, when we see something beautiful there is

1 Irving Sandler, *Abstract Expressionism and the American Experience: A Reevaluation*, Mission Critical Series, Lenox, MA: Hard Press Editions; New York: School of Visual Arts; in association with Hudson Hills Press, Manchester, VT, 2009, p. 25.

2 Elizabeth Schellekens, "Conceptual Art," October 2014, *Stanford Encyclopedia of Philosophy Archive*, http://plato.stanford.edu/archives/win2014/entries/conceptual-art.

3 Alexander Nehamas, *Only a Promise of Happiness: The Place of Beauty in a World of Art*, Princeton, NJ: Princeton University Press, 2007, p. 393.

4 Elizabeth K. Meyer, "Sustaining Beauty: The Performance of Appearance; A Manifesto in Three Parts," *Journal of Landscape Architecture*, Spring 2008, p. 9.

5 Ibid., p. 17.

104
Domenico Ghirlandaio.
Portrait of an Old Man and a Boy, ca. 1490.
[Public domain, United States]

a "willingness of the beholder to place himself or herself in the service of bringing new beauty into the world, creating a site of beauty separate from the self."[6] When we declare something beautiful, it makes us pause as we attempt to understand others—a crucial step to empathy. Scarry also contends that when we experience something beautiful, we are compelled to replicate it. "Beauty brings copies of itself into being. It prompts us to draw it, take a photograph of it, or describe it to other people. Sometimes it gives rise to exact replication and still other times to things whose connection to the original site of inspiration is unrecognizable."[7]

Another advocate of beauty and its resurrection in everyday life is Alexander Nehamas, whose theories deem something beautiful when it prompts us to seek more knowledge about it. For Nehamas, beauty is subjective and changes with time, and is everything we love, that we are drawn to and fascinated by.[8] Beauty is experienced when we interpret something in a work of art or culture. According to Nehamas, beauty can also operate when an aspect of something, such as a painting, is ugly. Moreover, interpretations do not always need to be intellectual endeavors; they can also communicate feelings. This happens in Domenico Ghirlandaio's *Old Man with a Child* [**104**]. The beauty Nehamas finds in the painting is not achieved through its formal qualities, but rather by the feelings it evokes. "The tenderness of the look the grandfather and grandchild so exchange is poignant precisely because the man's ugly nose does not come between them."[9] The child loves him despite the way he looks and this feeling of love conveyed in Ghirlandaio's depiction is what renders *Old Man with a Child* a beautiful painting. In short, when we are attracted to or drawn to beauty, we want to know more about it—this is the way in which beauty functions as an aspect of Claude Cormier's work.

This revival of beauty provides explanations that are not exclusively formalist—i.e., a conclusion based on color, line, or form. In other words, a landscape does not have to look beautiful to be experienced as beautiful.

6 Elaine Scarry, *On Beauty and Being Just*, Princeton, NJ: Princeton University Press, 1999, p. 117.

7 Ibid., p. 3.

8 Nehamas, *Only a Promise of Happiness*, p. 96.

9 Ibid.

105
Pink Balls.
Montréal, Québec, 2012.
View looking down
Sainte-Catherine
Street East.
[Guillaume Paradis,
Claude Cormier
et Associés]

106
Dorchester Square.
Montréal, Québec, 2010.
View showing new paving
at Dorchester Square.
[Marc Cramer]

107
Martha Schwartz,
The Bagel Garden.
Boston, Massachusetts, 1979.
[© Martha Schwartz Partners]

That said, many of Cormier's landscapes are formally beautiful. The projects from his fun side often transform objects with painting techniques such as illusion, color contrasts, and pointillism. The beauty of these projects at times derives from these techniques, but also stems from the projects' ability to communicate something about the site or context. An underlying premise of all Claude Cormier et Associés' work: to create a narrative that has meaning rooted in a place and its history. Certainly, many of the heritage projects express the less sanguine dimension of his work as they attempt to communicate a hidden or unofficial history of a site. In doing so, they also prompt our fascination and interpretation. Not all gardens and landscapes must hold meaning, but Cormier's surely do. At times they yell, "Hey, look at me," like the Lipstick Forest and Pink Balls [**105**]. At other times they offer only a quiet hint, such as the Place d'Armes and Dorchester Square—but they always have something to say, and this is an important facet of their beauty [**106**].

Objects of Affection

Claude Cormier's projects often evoke formalist ideals of beauty, but they also embody Nehamas's conceptions of beauty that build upon interpretations and evoked feelings, as well as Scarry's theory that beauty prompts replication. One of Cormier's chief techniques in attaining this beauty derives from his fondness for objects and his subsequent transformation of them. Whether colorful balls, painted stakes, or temporary overlay markers (TOMs), Cormier has employed some unlikely objects as design features in his gardens and landscapes. One of the earliest instances of this approach in landscape architecture was, of course, The Bagel Garden designed by Cormier's mentor, Martha Schwartz. Strategically located in her front yard, The Bagel Garden contained ninety-six lacquered bagels (a mixture of salt and pumpernickel) in a grid pattern upon a ground of colored gravel of the kind normally seen in hobby aquariums [**107**]. Schwartz argued that bagels were perfect for this north-facing small urban site and that they were shade tolerant, inexpensive, locally available, and required little maintenance. The Bagel Garden appeared on the cover of the 1980 January issue of *Landscape Architecture* magazine. In the accompanying article, Schwartz professed that she liked plants, but in some locations plants were just too difficult to maintain. "Having a landscape is like having a pet. You have to feed it. If you can't, get a stuffed animal," she recommended—advice Claude Cormier would heed thirty years later—*Les Peluches* (*Stuffed Animals*).[10]

10 Tim Richardson, *The Vanguard Landscapes and Gardens of Martha Schwartz*, London: Thames & Hudson, 2004, p. 149.

For some, bagels were deemed an inappropriate material for a garden. Yet Schwartz didn't want people planting bagels in their gardens; rather, she wanted to expand the material palette of landscape architects beyond plants. To that end, she also sought to make evident to the public that humans deliberately designed gardens and landscapes, and that these designs were as much cultural endeavors as other art practices. While Schwartz's work is considerably different today, her early work paved the way for Cormier's own approach to design. In fact, Cormier briefly worked for Schwartz and experienced firsthand the hard-won battles she fought to realize her ideas. Reflecting on his work with Schwartz in the early 1990s, Cormier remarked, "The experience in Martha's office demystified the star system to me. Practice is not easy; you need to convince people about things they don't know about, and not just do what they ask. You need to learn how to trust your own intuition. Watching Martha was great. She always stood up for what she believed in. She taught me an attitude with humor and compassion."[11]

Although respectful of Schwartz's design work, Cormier has developed a slightly different approach from his mentor. Like Schwartz, Cormier utilizes objects (particularly in his temporary works) from everyday life not typically employed as materials in designed landscapes. However, in many instances he transforms these items in ways that change our perception of the landscape and communicate knowledge about its setting. This approach differs slightly from Schwartz's work. At The Bagel Garden, the bagels remain bagels (albeit with lacquer). One of Cormier's most prevalent methods of transformation is, not surprisingly, color.

According to Cormier, "We realized early on that color is actually extremely loaded and we challenged that aspect within each project. I like to challenge preconceived ideas of color."[12] Indeed, in Cormier's hands, the use of color in itself becomes a method, a way of transforming objects that relay a specific narrative about its context. From the Op Art provocations of Blue Stick Garden to the alluring dollops of color produced by the stuffed animals of *Les Peluches* to the intricate pointillism of his TOM series, Cormier transforms objects into brushstrokes that challenge both our perception and our understanding of a place. What follows is a chronology of projects that demonstrate Cormier's consistent use of color to transform objects. Some of these earliest experiments began with interventions in the public spaces of Montréal.

Blue Lawn

Blue Lawn (1996–1997) was created in response to an upcoming 1998 Canadian Centre for Architecture (CCA) exhibition that featured photographs and discursive ephemera devoted to the American lawn. The Montréal exhibition examined Americans' rather obsessive relationship with lawns; their care, the activities they afford, and the power and pride they signal to others. When Cormier was a student at Harvard University, he read a *New York Times* article attesting to an absurd landscape practice of an American airport that painted its lawn areas with green paint when the grass turned yellow during the summer. He kept the newspaper article, thinking that the bizarre idea of painting grass might come in handy someday, and indeed, Cormier has employed this tactic in several other projects in addition to Blue Lawn.

As it happens, the lawns around the CCA, where he was providing landscape

11 Claude Cormier, interview with Susan Herrington, 6 April 2018.

12 Emily Waugh, "Interview with Claude Cormier + Associates," *Landscape Architecture's Core?*, Special issue, *Harvard Design Magazine* 36, 2013, p. 46.

108
Canadian Centre for Architecture landscape. Montréal, Québec, 1990. View of winter burn of grass areas.
[© CCA]

109
Blue Lawn.
Montréal, Québec, 1996.
Blue Lawn experiment.
[Claude Cormier
et Associés]

110
Blue Lawn.
Green blades taking
over blue blades.
[Claude Cormier
et Associés]

111
(opposite)
Blue Lawn.
Original concept
for Blue Lawn.
[Claude Cormier
et Associés]

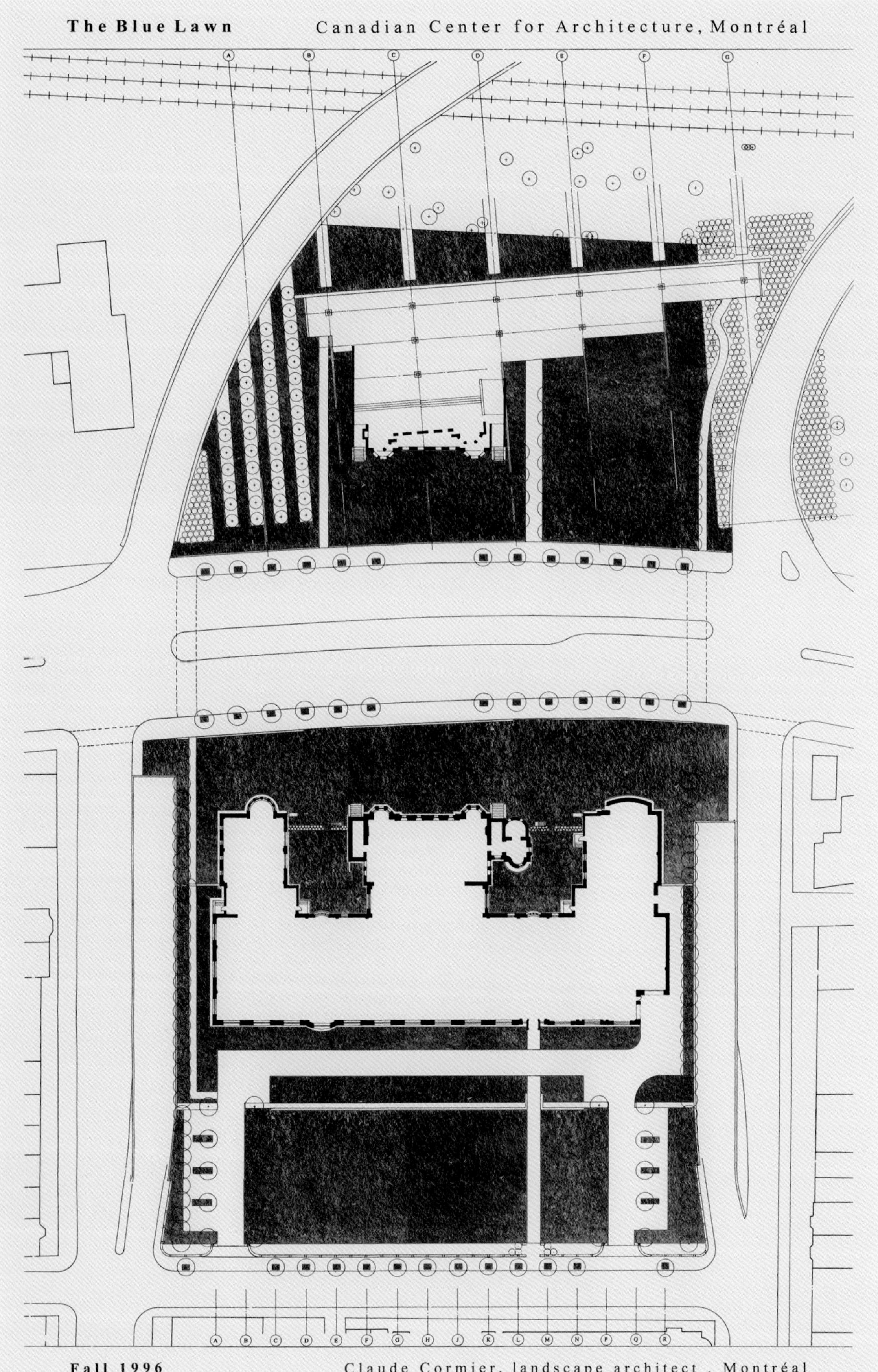
The Blue Lawn
Canadian Center for Architecture, Montréal
A
B
C
D
E
F
G
A
B
C
D
E
F
G
H
J
K
L
M
N
P
Q
R
Fall 1996
Claude Cormier, landscape architect , Montréal

112
Blue Lawn.
Montréal, Québec, 1996.
Exhibited Blue Lawn.
[Claude Cormier
et Associés]

architecture services, were yellow due to a harsh winter burn [108]. After experimenting with nontoxic Benjamin Moore paint and a patch of grass in his own backyard, Cormier managed to determine the proper mix of paint for turning the grass blue [109]. The shift in color would last approximately two weeks, after which the tender green shoots would emerge and eventually overtake the blue blades [110]. Given the eight-month duration of the *American Lawn* exhibition and the extent of the CCA's lawns, the CCA decided not to paint the entire lawn area as originally planned [111]. Blue Lawn was ultimately executed as three test beds located on the plaza outside of the CCA: one test bed contained regular green grass; the other two were blue [112].

Cormier selected the color blue because the CCA's branding was and still is blue, and by presenting blue lawns paired with the supposedly "untouched" natural green lawn he sought to elevate the lawn from its usual position as background to the foreground of perception. He also heightened the reading of lawns as inherently artificial. Although many people view lawns as natural, or even as signs of nature, lawns are also products of culture, and the measures that we take to keep them looking "natural" can be toxic. As one architect surmised about Blue Lawn, "What we fail to recognize is the negative environmental impact that lawns have: they deplete valuable water resources; they waste gas or electricity needed to maintain them; they are the grounds for the deployment of fertilizers and pesticides used to keep them green and healthy-looking."[13] While the architect's interpretation of Blue Lawn may not have been the exact message Cormier was attempting to send, the critic's desire to interpret the project and to take this interpretation a step further surely attests to the beauty offered by the cerulean-painted blades of grass. A year after Blue Lawn's installation, Cormier was given another opportunity to continue his experimentations. At the Jardins de Métis International Garden Festival he would produce one of his most celebrated works: Blue Stick Garden.

Blue Stick Garden

During the summer of 2000 in the remote wilds of the Gaspésie region of Québec, Cormier created a garden made of only painted wooden stakes. Blue Stick Garden was installed at the inaugural International Garden Festival at the Jardins de Métis/Reford Gardens. From *Gardens Illustrated* to the *New York Times*, dozens of articles reported on the festival and the questions provoked by the project. Must a garden contain plants to be considered a garden? Can painted sticks stand in for plants? Must gardens be composed of natural material? The repeated questions and opinions that Blue Stick Garden prompted are a credit to the project's beauty. As Nehamas suggests, beauty prompts us to want to know more, to interpret.

Blue Stick Garden comprised 3,500 garden stakes, each painted blue on three sides and orange on the fourth. The height and arrangement of the stakes were patterned after the Long Walk perennial border garden designed by Elsie Reford for the Edwardian garden adjacent to the festival site. In 1961 the Québec government acquired the garden for touristic purposes, and thirty-four years later the Reford Gardens was designated a national historic site of Canada. At this time, Alexander Reford, cofounder and director of the garden festival, began restoring his great-grandmother's gardens, which had fallen victim to neglect under their previous ownership. Fortunately, Elsie Reford had kept meticulous notes on her gardening activity,

13 Owen Rose, "Claude Cormier," *The Fifth Column* 10, no. 4, 2002, p. 27.

and her husband had documented the fruits of her labor in numerous photographs, which guided the garden's restoration. Indeed, the restored gardens, particularly The Long Walk, would captivate Cormier's imagination.

In preparation for the festival in 2000, Cormier, and the other selected designers, toured the newly restored Reford Gardens. They were also introduced to the dazzling Himalayan blue poppy (*Meconopsis betonicifolia*), which was in bloom that August day [113]. Discovered in Tibet in 1926 by the British plant hunter F. Kingdon Ward, the Himalayan blue poppy was highly sought after for its "unnatural" azure color. Elsie Reford's successful domestication of the Himalayan blue poppy was her most prized feat and the flower became emblematic of the Reford Gardens and Festival and a color guide for Cormier.

Alexander Reford's tour of his great-grandmother's garden concluded with The Long Walk that was inspired by the perennial borders pioneered by the British gardener Gertrude Jekyll. A key strategy of a perennial border garden is the blooming time and sequencing of color, as Jekyll acknowledges in her book *Colour in the Flower Garden*: "Even when a flower border is devoted to a special season, as mine is given to the time from mid-July to October, it cannot be kept fully furnished without resorting to various contrivances. One of these is the planting of certain things that will follow in season of bloom and that can be trained to take each other's places."[14]

In Reford's restored Long Walk, over 400 species and varieties of plants bloom in succession and change in hues from delicate yellow and white in the early spring, to pinks in mid-summer, to the blues and purples dominating the color display at summer's end [114]. Cormier was very taken with the gardening tradition of The Long Walk, and at the end of the tour he surprisingly announced that he would create a garden like Elsie Reford's Long Walk—but without using plants.

113
Jardins de Métis/
Reford Gardens
Grand-Métis, Québec, 2000.
Blue poppy in the
Blue Poppy Glade.
[Archives, Jardins de Métis]

On one hand, it makes sense not to use plants in a temporary garden located in a region where snow can remain as late as June and can return as early as October. The limited time available for installation and growth is insufficient for plants to reach maturity. On the other hand, it was difficult to visualize back in 1999 how Cormier's use of common garden stakes and paint could effect such a sensational garden experience—one that has never been adequately captured by the camera. Building Blue Stick Garden took weeks of grueling work. The stakes were painted blue by placing them in a cement mixer with blue paint. The gardeners painted the orange side of the stakes

114
Jardins de Métis/
Reford Gardens
Grand-Métis, Québec, 1999.
Elsie Reford's restored
Long Walk.
[Claude Cormier et Associés]

in situ. When gardeners erected Blue Stick Garden, one could hear their continual anguished cries (although these exclamations may have been due to the relentless black flies).

By 21 June, the opening day of the festival, the hard work of the gardeners had paid off in achieving Cormier's vision. Entering Blue Stick Garden, a linear space defined by the stakes, one is surrounded by blue, the collective hue of the painted stakes. Similar to a border perennial garden, the shorter stakes are placed at the edges of the pathway with taller stakes placed farther away [**115**]. As you turn to leave, however, your eyes are exposed to the fourth orange side of the stakes and the entire garden appears orange. Blue Stick Garden's tangy optical snap was one of Cormier's earliest works that transformed common objects, garden stakes, with paint to create a color illusion that tracks with the movement of the eye. As Scarry reminds us, sometimes replication can be unrecognizable. In other words, replication is not always exact. Both Reford's Long Walk and Cormier's Blue Stick Garden are beholden to the viewer's perceptual response and draw their inspiration from color theories that unite visual perception with visceral reaction. Yet Cormier substitutes the movement of seasons marked by plant growth and blooming times in Reford's perennial garden with the movement of the body and the eye [**116**] [**117**].

Blue Stick Garden set the stage for Cormier's particular brand of practice—his affection for objects from everyday life and his love of the transformative powers of color. In keeping with Scarry's idea that beauty brings copies of itself, Blue Stick Garden has been resurrected five times to date: in Montréal, Winnipeg, and Toronto, and in 2018 as a mobile garden set atop of a flatbed truck with a DJ sitting at its center in Montréal's Pride Parade. Its most sensational resurrection, however, was in 2004 at Hestercombe Gardens in Somerset, England, the iconic Edwardian garden designed by Gertrude Jekyll [**118**]. Interestingly, when Blue Stick Garden was constructed for its appearance at Hestercombe, there was no budget to return the stakes to Canada, so they found a second life as fencing material in numerous English domestic gardens after the garden was dismantled [**119**]. While each of Blue Stick Garden's reincarnations has changed slightly in layout, the transformation of the garden stakes in blue and orange has remained a constant. The blue and orange, of course, are emblematic of the Himalayan blue poppy and the Reford Gardens. If you look closely at the flower in bloom, bright orange anthers emerge from its center.

14 Gertrude Jekyll, *Colour in the Flower Garden*, The "Country Life" Library, London: "Country Life"; George Newnes, 1908, http://www.gutenberg.org/files/50764/50764-h/50764-h.htm.

115
Blue Stick Garden. Jardins de Métis/Reford Gardens, Québec, 2000. Orange and blue sticks of the Blue Stick Garden. [Claude Cormier et Associés]

116
Blue Stick Garden.
Jardins de Métis/Reford Gardens, Québec, 2000.
Blue side of the Blue Stick Garden in winter.
[Robert Baronet]

117
Blue Stick Garden.
Jardins de Métis/Reford
Gardens, Québec, 2000.
Orange side of the Blue
Stick Garden in winter.
[Robert Baronet]

118
Blue Stick Garden.
Hestercombe Gardens,
Taunton, England, 2004.
Peeking over the
wall of Gertrude Jekyll's
garden.
[Lynn Keddie]

119
Reuse of Blue Stick Garden
sticks in a domestic
garden.
Taunton, England.
[Photographer unknown]

Lipstick Forest

Blue Stick Garden helped launch Claude Cormier's reputation as a rule breaker and a landscape architect who exploited color and its agency—and as a designer with no qualms about enlisting unconventional objects as part of his material palette. In this regard Lipstick Forest does not disappoint. In 1998, Cormier was asked to design a winter garden for the newly expanded Palais des congrès convention center in the heart of Montréal. While the clients had envisioned plants for the winter garden, Cormier chided them, remarking that interior plants are what you see in shopping malls, not in a major international convention center. One sentiment that Cormier and the client agreed upon was the fact that the long, gray winters in Montréal contribute to a depressed mood among the public. In response, Cormier combined two seemingly distant elements—glossy pink paint and the stately beauty of trees—to create fifty-two lipstick tree trunks in luscious pink.

The shapes of the trees' trunks were drawn from photographs of silver maples (*Acer saccharinum*) that once graced the streets of Montréal [120]. Trees throughout Montréal had been heavily damaged by the 1998 ice storm and Cormier sought to remind us of their once-grand presence in the city. Because the drawings traced only the shapes of the tree trunks and a branch or two (and not their textured bark or dense branching pattern), the trees of Lipstick Forest are abstract versions of the photographs of trees. They were fabricated with gunite (a slurry of cement, sand, and water applied through a pressure hose) over a wire mesh and metal frame. A high gloss fluorescent pink covered these gunite creations. In keeping with his concern for visual perception, Cormier selected fluorescent pink so that the trees would be vivid from the outside looking into the Palais's interior spaces. According to Cormier, when you look inside a building, dark objects are barely noticeable, so to make the trees visible, he selected the shocking pink.[15]

Like Blue Lawn and Blue Stick Garden, Lipstick Forest stresses the artificial over the fake as the more authentic response to the design brief. To Cormier, "fake" describes a material that is meant to deceive, to look indistinguishable from something it is not. Artificial turf, for example, is fake. For Cormier, "Artificial still refers to something authentic…like a canopy of trees in a forest, even if it's a sky-blue canopy made of fibreglass."[16] Here, Cormier refers to another example of artificial over fake, the project Blue Forest [121]. Located in a linear courtyard of Nissan's design studio in Detroit, Blue Forest comprises a suspended canopy of branches painted blue [122]. The company was so enchanted with Blue Forest that when Nissan was forced to close their Detroit studio in 2009, they relocated Blue Forest to their offices in La Jolla, California [123].

Yet can something fake be authentic? The work *Magnolias for Pittsburgh* (2006), by the artist Tony Tasset, provides a useful comparison to explore this question. For a small park, Tasset created two magnolia trees cast in bronze, with both trees based on the exact measurements of a magnolia tree he discovered while walking his dog. The trees were hand-painted with 800 individually rendered petals. In the small park that was the site of the project, five real-life magnolia trees were planted around the tree sculptures. During the spring months, when the real trees are in bloom, it is almost impossible to tell the difference between Tasset's fake magnolia trees and the living trees. Tasset's trees are a good fake; Cormier's tree trunks are artificial.

15 Cormier, interview with Herrington, 18 August 2018.

16 Waugh, "Interview," p. 46.

120
Lipstick Forest.
Montréal, Québec, 1996.
Photos of trees in
Montréal and Lipstick
Forest.
[Jean-François Vézina
and Claude Cormier
et Associés]

121
Blue Forest.
Farmington Hills,
Michigan, 2007.
Construction of
Blue Forest;
photo taken in 2004.
[Claude Cormier
et Associés]

122
(opposite)
Blue Forest.
Blue Forest at the
Nissan Design Studio.
[François Farion]

123
(opposite)
Blue Forest.
Farmington Hills,
Michigan, 2007.
Blue Forest at the
Nissan Design Studio.
[Joshua Willerton]

124
Lipstick Forest.
Montréal, Québec, 1996.
Lipstick Forest up close.
[Jean-François Vézina]

125
Sugar Beach.
Toronto, Ontario, 2010.
Sugary fountain.
[Nicola Betts]

126
(opposite)
Sugar Beach.
Toronto, Ontario, 2010.
Hard rock candy.
[Claude Cormier
et Associés]

127
Sugar Beach.
Vent pipe as candy cane.
[Nicola Betts]

Is there something profoundly artificial about the color pink? Does Cormier like pink because he's gay? And if pink, which pink? Baker-Miller pink is produced by mixing one pint of red semigloss outdoor trim paint and one gallon of pure white indoor latex paint (think Pepto-Bismol). In 1979, United States naval officers found that exposure to this color reduced the aggressive and violent behavior of inmates in a correctional facility.[17] However, the pink of Cormier's trees is not Baker-Miller pink, which is high in tonal value (lighter) and weak in chroma (hue saturation). In contrast, the pink at Lipstick Forest is not as high in tonal value while it is more saturated in chroma [124].

Cormier uses pink as a contextual reference as well. At Sugar Beach in Toronto, for example, thirty-six pink umbrellas dot the beach, looking like Canada Mints in Wintergreen (the candies are actually pink) sprinkled across an expanse of sugary sand. The confectionery allure of pink umbrellas speaks to the Redpath Sugar Refinery situated across the slip (a refinery that still emits a sugar mist that at times wafts across the site today) [125]. Cormier even extended his references to sugar beyond color at Sugar Beach. He relentlessly searched for beach sand that had a sugary white texture and color, and the candy-striped granite rock outcropping—a genuine geological curiosity—connotes the hard rock candies of times past [126]. Even the stainless steel ventilation pipe to the fountain is etched to resemble a candy cane [127].

Similar to his choices at Sugar Beach, Cormier employs the color pink to communicate to us something about the context in which he is working. Cormier himself has said that the pink at Lipstick Forest was inspired the city's famed "pink kiss"—unfortunately, like the storm-ravaged silver maple trees, the logo has been kissed goodbye as the branding image for Tourisme Montréal [128]. And in this sense, the forest speaks to contemporary commercial life. There is a sense too that Lipstick Forest challenges the traditional definitions of a landscape as a tranquil scene of untouched nature. Its artificiality and just-applied look demonstrate that landscapes today are part of mass culture, and thus they are commercial, market-driven, swayed by desire, and perhaps subjected to as much niche marketing as lipstick itself.

Lipstick Forest opened in 2002 with the inauguration of the Palais des congrès. Like Blue Stick Garden, it received extensive press coverage, but the initial responses were…well, not uniformly positive. The project appeared on the cover of *Le Journal de Montréal* with the headline in 48-point type, "C'est Horrible !" uttered by Frédéric Metz, founding member of the Centre de design de l'Université du Québec à

128
Kiss logo.
Montréal, Québec, 2004.
Inspiration for Lipstick Forest.
[Claude Cormier et Associés, Paprika]

Montréal.[18] Despite initial lambasting, Lipstick Forest grew, so to speak, on the people of Montréal and its visitors.[19] It has even inspired people to think about new ways of decorating. In a 2009 What's Now feature, "Nature Inspired Interiors," the *Elle Decor* (*India*) editor Pragnya Rao wrote, "Think Pink. Picture this: 52 concrete trees painted lipstick pink and patterned after century-old maples that lined the avenues of old Montréal. Gorgeous, isn't it?"[20]

Cormier's pink trees have lasted close to twenty years, a point that he likes to drive home. During a visit in 2017, the Palais des congrès was hosting the ninth annual Comic-Con. Approximately 56,000 people dressed as superheroes and science fiction characters infiltrated the Palais. Befittingly, a Wolverine and two Ninja Turtles decided to take a break from the frenetic action in the exhibition hall to partake of a picnic lunch among the trees of the Lipstick Forest.

Blue Tree

Blue Tree, created in 2004 for the Cornerstone Festival of Gardens in Sonoma, California, continued the practice of transforming objects with color, except with Blue Tree, Cormier created an entirely new object—the unlikely crossing of a ping-pong ball with a blue Christmas tree ornament. Cormier had often professed that when he was studying agronomy, he wanted to breed a new type of flower. For Blue Tree he managed to invent a hybrid that crossbred the best traits of both objects: the lightweight durability of a ping-pong ball with the built-in hanging capabilities of a Christmas tree ornament.

Why cover a tree with blue plastic balls? Cormier intentionally selected the garden plot because it contained a Monterey pine tree that stood sixty feet tall—and the tree was dying. Cormier likes constraints, and a large dying tree served up the perfect limitation for his temporary garden. His response was to chop down the tree—at least virtually. Working with a Photoshop digital image of the garden site, Cormier's team used the color replacement brush and the match-color tools to replicate a brush dot in the same hue of the Sonoma sky [129]. In the process, they in effect camouflaged the tree in the digital image. This visual investigation led him to his response for the festival plot—to literally cover the dying tree with 70,000 spherical blue ornaments in order to make it disappear against the sky.

The setting for Blue Tree could not have been more dissimilar to the garden festival in Québec, the site of the Blue Stick Garden, which he had participated in four years earlier. Situated on the dusty outskirts of Sonoma, in a region where the temperature rarely ventures beyond 90 degrees Fahrenheit in the summer or below 45 degrees Fahrenheit in the winter, the Cornerstone Gardens site was warm and dry. Compared to the Québec garden festival site, where the plots for the temporary gardens were literally carved out of the dense spruce forests, the Sonoma festival site was also quite exposed, save for the dying tree.

Cornerstone opened its nine-acre garden festival in 2004 with sixteen garden installations.[21] While Cormier had concealed the tree in its digital representation, its three-dimensional presence was anything but

17 James E. Gilliam, "The Effects of Baker-Miller Pink on Physiological and Cognitive Behavior of Emotionally Disturbed and Regular Education Students," *Behavioral Disorders* 17, no. 1, 1991, p. 47.

18 Claude Cormier, "Color Is Not a Decoration," P. H. Elwood Lecture, Iowa State University, 17 October 2014, https://vimeo.com/109731946.

19 David Theodore, "Bright Lights, Big Price Tag: The New Palais des congrès Is Worth Every Cent," *Maisonneuve*, 1 March 2003, https://maisonneuve.org/article/2003/03/1/bright-lights-big-price-tag/.

20 Pragnya Rao, "Nature Inspired Interiors: Out in the Open," What's Now: Design, Architecture & Art, *Elle Decor* (*India*), April—May 2009, p. 82.

21 See Chris Hougie, *Cornerstone: Festival of Gardens; New Frontiers in Modern Gardens,* Novato, CA: ORO Editions, 2005.

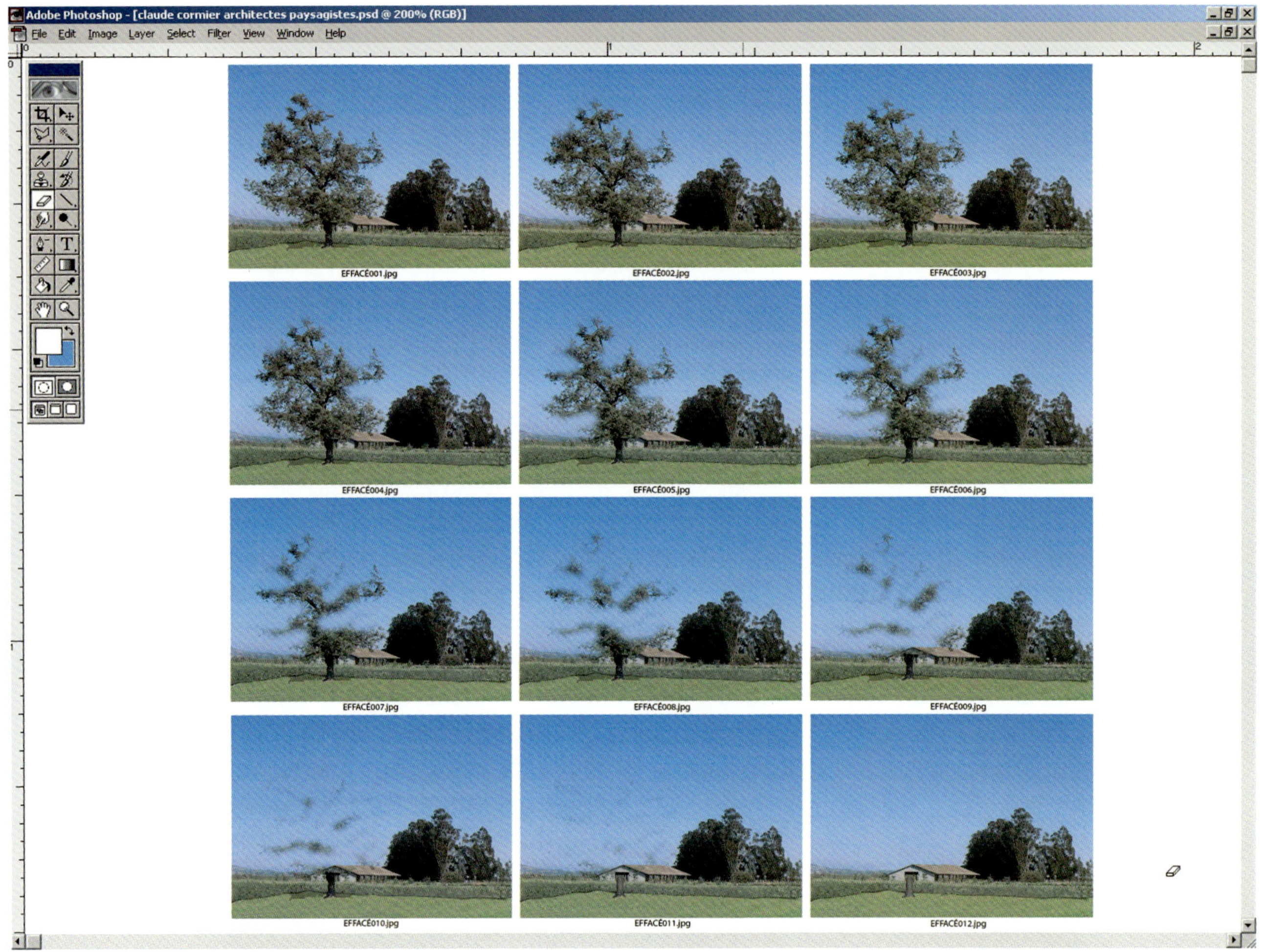

129
Blue Tree.
Sonoma, California, 2004.
The tree vanishes
with Photoshop.
[Claude Cormier
et Associés]

130
(opposite)
Blue Tree.
Blue Tree on opening day.
[Cornerstone Gardens]

131
Blue Tree.
Sonoma, California, 2004.
Blue Tree close-up.
[Geneviève L'Heureux]

camouflaged [130]. The scale of the tree, and its position in the open landscape, as well as its unique form, made it visible even before entering the garden area. Similar to what was done at the French garden festival at Chaumont, the organizers envisioned that hedges would define each of the gardens, but in 2004 the newly planted shrubs offered no spatial definition for the plots, making Blue Tree highly visible.

Blue Tree's location, but also the curious blue ball ornaments and how they draped around the tree's limbs like the DNA chains of a Dr. Seuss character, made it emblematic for the festival [131]. Blue Tree appeared on the cover of promotional material and it was the visual focus of many reviews of the Cornerstone Festival. Blue Tree even appeared on the cover of a philosophy book, *Knowing Art: Essays in Aesthetics and Epistemology*, published in 2006.[22] Hardly concealed against the Sonoma skies, the tree remained on the festival site for three years. Indeed, transforming the dying tree with a shade of blue based on the California sky draws attention to its formal qualities, its height, its shape (pruned by Cormier), and the festival site's former life as humble agricultural lands.

Les Peluches (Stuffed Animals)

A less publicized Cormier project, and occupying an interior space, is *Stuffed Animals*. In 2011 the Montreal Museum of Fine Arts launched an exhibition entitled *Big Bang* to celebrate the creative process with the idea that the initial galactic event represented "the absolute symbol of creation: a mysterious creation and very old, yet still alive."[23] To this end, twenty verifiably creative people, who ranged from architects to fashion designers to jugglers, were asked to select a piece from the permanent collection of the museum and respond to it. Just the year before, Claude Cormier was involved in a participatory exhibition at the McCord Museum in Montréal entitled *90 Treasures, 90 Stories, 90 Years*, where artists selected works from the collection and then created YouTube presentations explaining why they thought the selected work was important.[24] For *Big Bang*, however, the curators took this idea a step further and asked the participants to create an entirely new work that responded to the artwork they had selected.

Cormier, the only landscape architect participating, chose a limestone sculpture, *Head of an Apostle*, found in Burgundy, France, that dated to approximately 1150 CE. Building upon the feeling of adoration and the veneration of Christ imparted by this sculpture, Cormier reflected on his own adoration of animals, particularly his love of plush toy animals. He had grown up with animals but was too busy to keep a pet as an adult. Perhaps taking Martha Schwartz's advice, for over a year, on every Saturday, he began patronizing vintage stores in Montréal (the Renaissance store was the best) to buy used stuffed animals.[25] By year's end he had collected over 3,500 stuffed animals in a multitude of colors.

The key to the transformation of these objects of adoration was their treatment as

22 Dominic Lopes and Matthew Kieran, eds., *Knowing Art: Essays in Aesthetics and Epistemology*, Philosophical Studies Series 107, Dordrecht: Springer Netherlands, 2006, cover and back.

23 *Big Bang—Giving Free Rein to Creativity* (*Big Bang—Carte blanche à la créativité*), Montreal Museum of Fine Arts, https://translate.google.com/translate? hl=en&sl=fr&u=https://voir.ca/bigbang/2011/11/08/big-bang-carte-blanche-a-la-creativite/&prev=search.

24 Claude Cormier, "*The Burning of the Canadian Parliament in Montréal*, 1849," McCord Museum, 17 March 2011, https://www.youtube.com/watch?v=2iedvsLhA1I.

25 Conversation, Claude Cormier, Georges-Étienne Parent, Marc Treib, and Susan Herrington, 8 July 2017, Montreal Museum of Fine Arts.

132
(opposite)
Les Peluches
(Stuffed Animals).
Montreal Museum
of Fine Arts.
Montréal, Québec, 2011.
Les Peluches
with Claude Cormier.
[Natasha Gysin]

133
Les Peluches
(Stuffed Animals).
Les Peluches with
Head of an Apostle.
[MMFA, Denis Farley]

134
Les Peluches
(Stuffed Animals).
Montreal Museum
of Fine Arts.
Montréal, Québec, 2011.
The full work.
[MMFA, Denis Farley]

dollops of colored paint characteristic of Abstract Expressionist paintings [132]. Trading colored stuffed animals for splotches of paint hue, Cormier arranged the toys by color to create areas of brown, gray, white, blue, yellow, green, purple, orange, and of course, pink, balanced across the canvas as perfectly as a Lee Krasner painting. Working with his friend, the artist Georges Audet, he stapled each stuffed animal at the neck to small panels of plywood that when put together created a sixteen-feet-long by eight-feet-high tableau.

When the exhibit opened in November of 2011, *Les Peluches* (*Stuffed Animals*) was affixed to the gallery wall directly facing a pedestal showcasing *Head of an Apostle* in an apparent stare-down [133]. While many visitors may have had difficulty finding the idea of adoration that linked the rather sullen-looking *Head of an Apostle* with the googly-eyed stuffed animals, they were mesmerized by the dazzling display of soft color—or as the writer Steven Howell commented, "All eyes from museum visitors on hand seem to be on that hypnotic wall of plush toys."[26] At show's end, *Stuffed Animals* became part of the museum's permanent collection and today it is located in the museum's newly expanded educational spaces for schoolchildren and families. The dazzling creatures greet visitors when they enter this new addition [134]. One can't help but touch this soft and colorful delight, and to be sure many children probably have been told to touch with their eyes only.

Temporary Overlay Markers (TOMs) Evolution

TOM I: Field of Daisies, 2012

The transformation of everyday objects using painterly color techniques is also evident in Cormier's TOM series. First created for the inauguration of the Montreal Museum of Fine Arts Sculpture Garden in 2012, the project was repeated four times, with the leitmotif changing each year. The TOM series converts the banal asphalt surface of the l'avenue du Musée in front of the museum into a color field by treating Temporary Overlay Markers (TOMs) as points of color. This half-block-long roadway links the museum's four major buildings: Montreal Museum of Fine Arts, pavillon Claire et Marc Bourgie, pavillon Jean-Noël Desmarais, and pavillon Michal et Renata Hornstein. As the street was closed to traffic in the summer, the museum curators assumed the city would surface the avenue with granite pavers to provide an exterior courtyard. Unfortunately, the city paved the road with only asphalt. Cormier was asked to intervene with a temporary design that would provide interest in the summer and speak to the art complexes that surrounded it, all accomplished with very little money or time.

A temporary overlay marker is four inches long and two inches high, and is made of a polyurethane material that affords substantial bending memory. They are typically arranged to delineate temporary lanes for drivers passing through construction zones. The idea of using TOMs came to Cormier several years earlier when driving in rural Québec to visit his mother. On that drive along freshly paved Highway 15, he kept noticing these little yellow and white tabs on the road. "I pulled over and got out of the car and bent over and ripped one off the asphalt road. I stuck it in my back pocket. I had a feeling these things might come in handy one day."[27] Like the newspaper article about painting grass he had once saved, he

26 Steven Howell, "Eclectic Installations," *Press-Republican*, 29 December 2011, http://www.pressrepublican.com/news/out_and__about/eclectic-installations/article_4fdc5ed5-f5d8-5f95-ac9b-bce808238ad4.html.

27 Cormier, interview with Herrington, 25 July 2018.

135
TOM I: Field of Daisies.
Montréal, Québec, 2012.
Plan view.
[Claude Cormier
et Associés]

136
TOM I: Field of Daisies. Montréal, Québec, 2012. Inspiration for Field of Daisies. [Zeynel Cebeci, Wikimedia Commons]

also kept the little TOM. When the director of the museum telephoned and sighed, "I want something fun, oh, and I have no money and I need it in two weeks," Cormier immediately knew how he would finally use that pilfered TOM.[28] By employing thousands of TOMs and changing their normal layout from a linear alignment to the pattern of a field, Cormier created a pixelated visual display that dazzled visitors to the l'avenue du Musée [135].

In 2012, the markers were manufactured in only two colors (yellow and white) so Cormier created Field of Daisies by affixing 3,500 yellow and white tabs to the asphalt road [136] [137]. The material was low in cost—a case of 500 markers was only $410 US. With blue chalk, Cormier's team stenciled a diagonal pattern on the roadway. Each TOM was positioned at the intersections of the chalked lines with the longer side of the TOM facing the viewer. Upon opening in the summer of 2012, the collective tableau of yellow and white tabs cohered as a color field that drew people into the closed street to inspect its surface further and stroll. As the TOMs were designed to endure wheeled vehicular traffic, they could surely withstand foot traffic and maintenance trucks. According to Cormier, Field of Daisies was a way of taking back the street for the summer, and it was so popular that he was asked to return the following year.

TOM II: Field of Poppies, 2013

In 2013 Cormier reconceived the same 3,767-square-foot asphalt surface in a second edition called Field of Poppies, in homage to Vincent van Gogh's rendering of poppy fields. By this time, the Seattle-based TOM manufacturer, which Cormier had used the year before, informed him that if he ordered a substantial numbers of TOMs the firm could produce them in any color of his choosing. In response, Cormier expanded the TOM color palette to include green and red, which he speckled with white TOMs to produce strong contrasts of color [138]. By mixing complementary colors, Cormier enhanced the resulting optical effects, much like illusionary techniques used in painting styles such as pointillism [139]. As a result, the dotted brush strokes of TOMs produced a vibrant scene [140]. As Michel-Eugène Chevreul reminds us in his Law of Simultaneous Contrast of Color, colors affect one another and "the optical composition of each juxtaposed colour" is most noticeable when complementary colors are placed side by side.[29] Field of Poppies also doubled the number of TOMs

28 Ibid.

29 Michel-Eugène Chevreul, "The Principles of Harmony and Contrast of Colours, and Their Applications to the Arts," in *Nineteenth-Century Theories of Art*, ed. Joshua C. Taylor, Berkeley: University of California Press, 1987, p. 452.

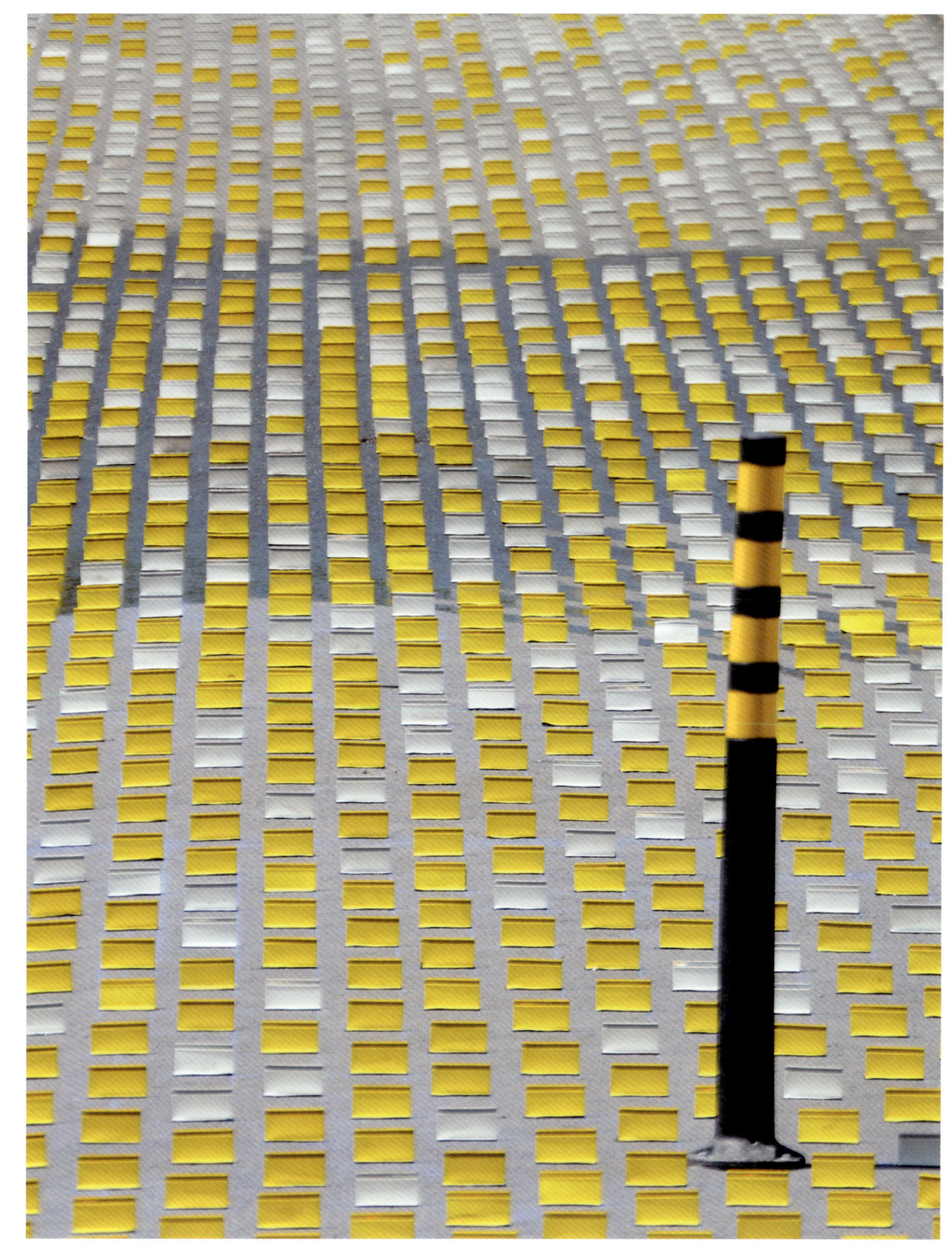

137
TOM I: Field of Daisies.
Montréal, Québec, 2012.
Street view.
[Guillaume Paradis, Claude
Cormier et Associés]

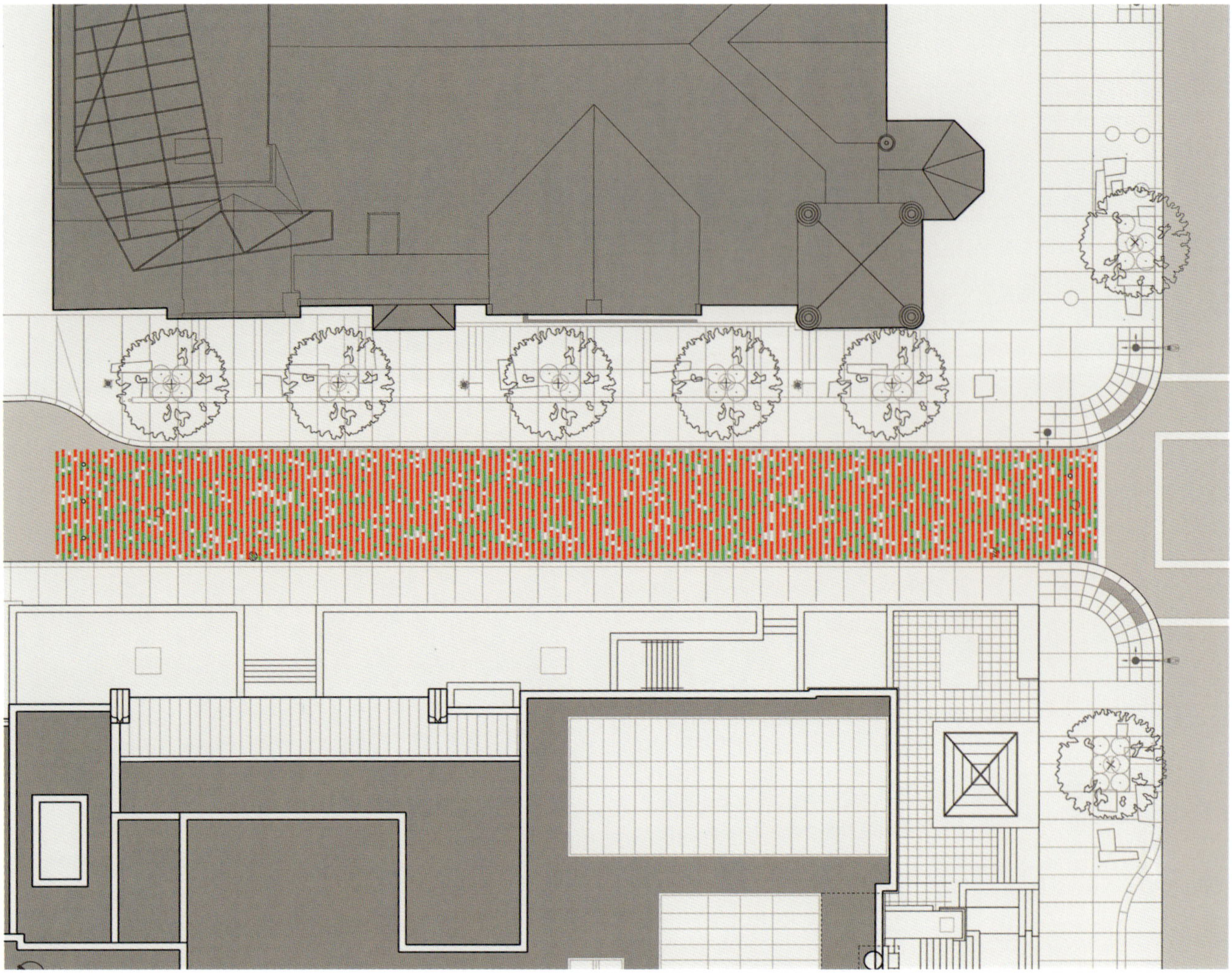

138
TOM II: Field of Poppies.
Montréal, Québec, 2013.
Plan view.
[Claude Cormier
et Associés]

139
TOM II: Field of Poppies.
Close-up view.
[Guillaume Paradis, Claude
Cormier et Associés]

140
(opposite)
TOM II: Field of Poppies.
Street view.
[Guillaume Paradis, Claude
Cormier et Associés]

MUSEUM OF FINE ARTS
M
PEROU

141
TOM III: Mirage.
Montréal, Québec, 2014.
Plan.
[Claude Cormier
et Associés]

142
(pages 190–191)
TOM III: Mirage.
Street view
approaching the museum
and leaving the museum.
[Guillaume Paradis, Claude
Cormier et Associés]

used—to 6,000—a density that also enhanced the chromatic and illusionary effects.

TOM III: Mirage, 2014

In the summer of 2014, another artist was commissioned to create the temporary installation at l'avenue du Musée. Unfortunately, or perhaps fortunately, the proposal was rejected and Claude Cormier was asked to step in at the last minute. Mirage referenced the jeweler-artist Peter Carl Fabergé, whose work had been exhibited at the Montreal Museum of Fine Arts that summer. TOM III: Mirage comprised a whopping 10,000 TOMs. The manufacturer had again expanded its color palette at Cormier's request, and each TOM was now backed with another TOM of a different color. This made Mirage one of the most visually fascinating iterations of the TOM evolution. The double-backed TOMs provided a different color scheme depending on which direction visitors walked down l'avenue du Musée [141].

Approaching TOM III from rue Sherbrooke, one was greeted with a dazzling field of blue, white, black, and yellow TOMs, the signature colors of the Tsarevich Egg created by Fabergé for Empress Alexandra Fyodorovna in 1912. Walking from l'avenue du Docteur-Penfield, one is transfixed by a vibrating scheme of yellow, red, orange, white, and purple TOMs, referencing another one of Fabergé's bejeweled creations [142]. The color pattern, too, was optically more complex than previous versions. At Mirage, groups of TOMs of the same color form overlapping diamond shapes that appear and disappear as one moves around the street [143].

TOM IV: Flower Power, 2017

The 2017 rendition represented a slightly different take on the temporary overlay marker series. Entitled Flower Power, TOM IV was created for the 375th anniversary of Montréal and the 50th anniversary of Expo 67, and also paid tribute to the city's 1960s counterculture. Here the TOMs swirl in a spiral pattern reminiscent of the iconic tie-dye technique favored by hippies [144]. Injected among the multitude of tabs was a new object: five pale-pink raised circular forms reminiscent of giant Ecstasy pills—given the time period, however, the reference was more likely LSD [145]. In place of an overall optical field condition, as in previous versions of the TOM series, the optical effects were sensed more individually, with different swirling forms emerging as one walked through the work.

A clue to the beauty of Cormier's work can be found in his transformation of objects that play with our perception and communicate a message about a place. This catalog of Cormier's affectionate treatment of objects has sought to reveal how many of his projects dazzle us with color illusions. Blue Stick Garden, Blue Tree, and the TOM series treat objects such as stakes, balls, and temporary overlay markers as points of color that lure us into the work and prompt us to ask what it all means. Within Scarry's conception of beauty, Cormier's projects also afford great social efficacy because they prompt exchange among people. The glossy pink tree trunks of Lipstick Forest and the soft array of toy animals of *Stuffed Animals* make us pause and try to figure out what Cormier is trying to convey; we might even ask a stranger what she thinks. The TOM series in particular exemplifies Nehamas's theory of beauty. Most people don't normally find temporary overlay markers beautiful. In Cormier's hands, however, the TOMs function collectively, in their colors and layout, as beautiful.

Informed by History

In many of Claude Cormier's designs for public spaces in Montréal, the site's history and historical features provide the mantle

QUEBEC AND CANADIAN ART
M
LES RENDEZ-VOUS
D'ART
CONTEM-PORAIN
lemieux pilon
1+1=1
MBAM+MAC

MUSÉE DES BEAUX-ARTS
M
JARDIN DE SCULPTURES
M
MUSEUM OF FINE ARTS
M
SCULPTURE GARDEN
M
Liliane et David M. Stewart

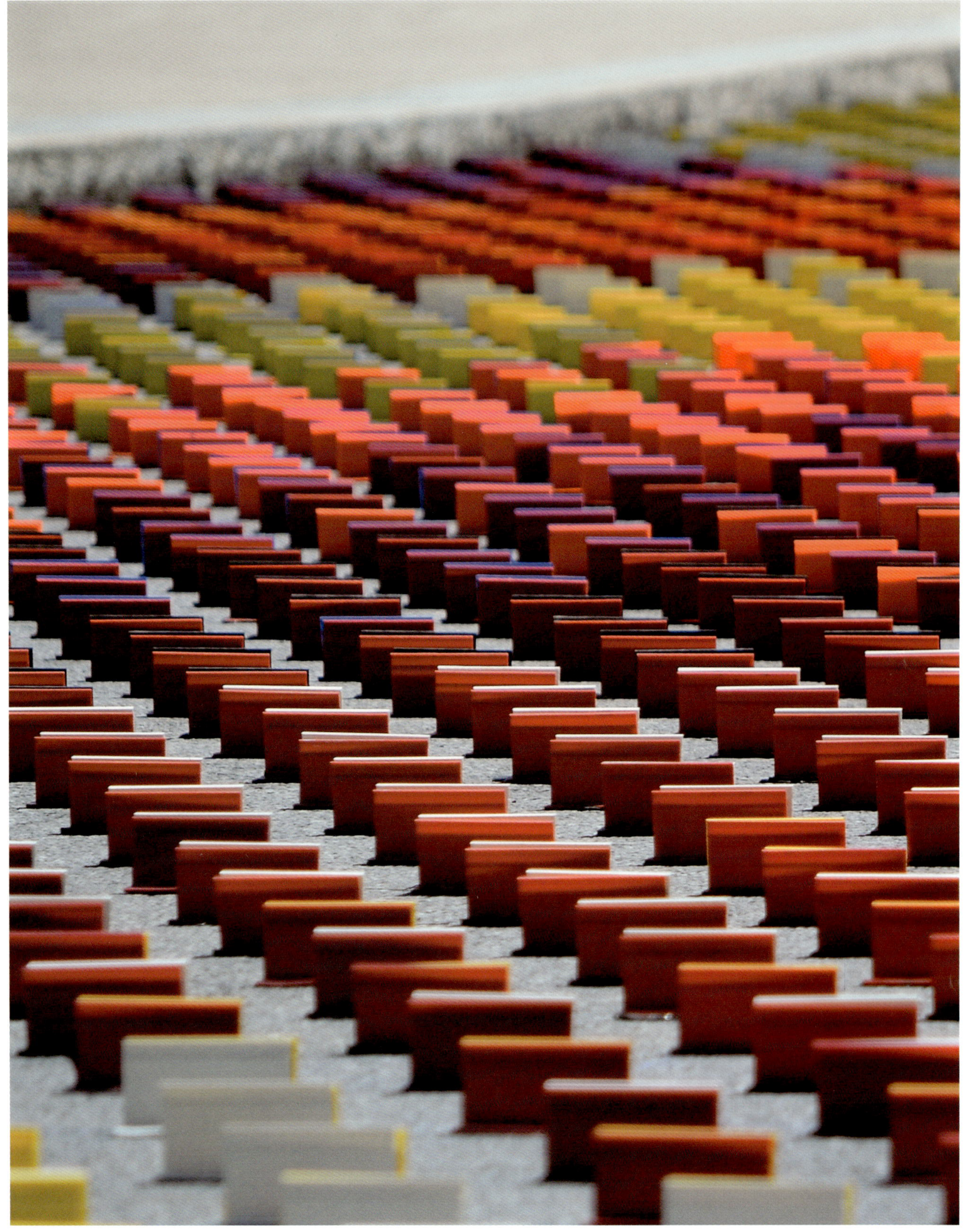

143
(opposite)
TOM III: Mirage.
Montréal, Québec, 2014.
Close-up view.
[Guillaume Paradis, Claude Cormier et Associés]

144
TOM IV: Flower Power.
Montréal, Québec, 2017.
Plan.
[Claude Cormier et Associés]

145
TOM IV: Flower Power.
Montréal, Québec, 2017.
Aerial view.
[MMFA, Denis Farley]

for his conceptual thinking and reveal his more serious side. Cormier's deep interest in history can be traced to his experiences at Harvard University as a master's student in the Graduate School of Design. During his first semester of study, he became increasingly disenchanted with the required reading assignments that included texts by Immanuel Kant, Martin Heidegger, Maurice Merleau-Ponty, and other philosophers. Cormier lamented, "I was not born to do this."[30] During his second semester, however, he took courses with the historians Mirka Beneš and John Stilgoe that sparked a deep respect for the work of Frederick Law Olmsted, Sr. For Cormier,

> *Reading, understanding, and appreciating the picturesque landscape—despite my wanting to be a contemporary designer—was a big inspiration during my time at the GSD. Understanding the role and interpretation of history was, and is still, a big influence on my thinking. I read Elizabeth K. Meyer who juxtaposed historical with contemporary landscape architecture. She was presenting and comparing Olmsted with Tschumi designers, who were 100 years apart. Beth helped me make connections that I never did before. She triggered my mind and made history huge to me. She was brilliant.*[31]

The juxtaposition of historical information with contemporary design deeply influenced Cormier after his return to Montréal. Reflecting upon this connection, he surmised, "It described the real connection of nature to the city. My past rural upbringing combined with a newfound, emerging knowledge of history have provided the underlying ideas for all of my work."[32] And what better place to explore these intersections than Montréal, a city steeped in French and English histories with their respective design traditions—differences that were, not surprisingly, expressed in the urban fabric.

Phillips Square

Phillips Square (1996–1997) in downtown Montréal represents one of Cormier's earliest heritage projects. It was also his first design to address the ground plane and its patterning as a means to express the history of the site, and thus, its beauty. The square's namesake, Thomas Phillips, has been described as a Devonshire man and "a building contractor and city councilor of Montréal."[33] Phillips had purchased the six-acre hilltop on the outskirts of Montréal in 1842 but died that same year. Martha Anderson, his widow, donated the land to the city, envisioning its development as a belvedere dedicated to her husband. Once considered on the outskirts of town, by the turn of the century the area had evolved into one of Montréal's wealthiest neighborhoods for Anglophones. A shopping district developed around the square, which was bordered by Sainte-Catherine Street West, Cathcart Street, Place Phillips, and Union Avenue.

In 1914 a monument to King Edward VII, modeled by sculptor Louis-Philippe Hébert, was installed in the middle of the square as its most prominent feature, becoming a source of inspiration for Cormier eight decades later. Cast in bronze, Edward VII stands upon a column on a terraced base with bronze allegorical figures gracing all four sides. During the 1930s, the city constructed a set of symmetrically placed staircases to the north of the monument

30 Cormier and Parent, interview with Treib and Herrington, 9 July 2017, Claude Cormier et Associés Offices, Montréal.

31 Ibid.

32 Ibid.

33 Alan Hustak, "Downtown Montréal—Phillips Square," Montréal Walking Tours, 2002, Véhicule Press, http://www.vehiculepress.com/Montréal/downtown.html.

that provided access to the subterranean lavatories. The addition of these washrooms pleased members of Québec's sovereignty movement, who thought it was only fitting that people might relieve themselves under the monument of Edward VII.

By the end of the 1970s the subterranean lavatories had devolved into places for nefarious activities; in response, the entrances were closed and turned into large planters. Despite the square's decline, by the 1990s the surrounding area had evolved into a fashionable shopping district. In 1996, Cormier, in collaboration with Bernard St-Denis, was commissioned to renovate the square. Their proposed paving scheme took its inspiration from an unusual source. Building upon Montréal's reputation as a hub for fashion and design, they focused on King Edward VII's penchant for designing and promoting men's suits and sportswear. As Cormier has noted, during the 1990s people didn't pay attention to King Edward VII as a historical figure or even as a feature of the square. However, during his lifetime, "he was [regarded as] a real dandy" who routinely changed his outfit six times a day.[34] The king was also known for his regionally based clothing [146]. He designed a special coat he called the Deeside, for example, which he wore while hunting on the castle grounds along the River Dee in Scotland.[35] Indeed, King Edward VII was a fitting muse for Cormier who also endeavored to express site specificity through his design work.

For the square's paving, Cormier reinterpreted the houndstooth pattern King Edward VII had personally promoted in his choice of suits and produced a series of drawings for the city's approval [147]. On a more whimsical note, Cormier also proposed that the washrooms be transformed into a nightclub. Unsurprisingly, the nightclub was not approved, but the implementation of the paving scheme did proceed. Unfortunately, a member of Heritage Montréal saw the drawings and expressed his horror at the idea [148]. As a result, the project died. Never parting from a good idea, however, Cormier managed to test the houndstooth pattern twenty years later at Le Château Apartments in Montréal, surely among the swankiest parking lots in existence [149].[36] Cormier learned from this public process as well. He discovered that he had to be more strategic to win people over to his ideas. Phillips Square also brought to light the importance of the ground plane in referencing the history of a site, an idea that would manifest itself at Place d'Youville a year later.

146
King Edward VII.
King of England, 1901-1910.
[AF archive / Alamy Stock Photo]

147
Houndstooth pattern.
Samples.
[Claude Cormier et Associés]

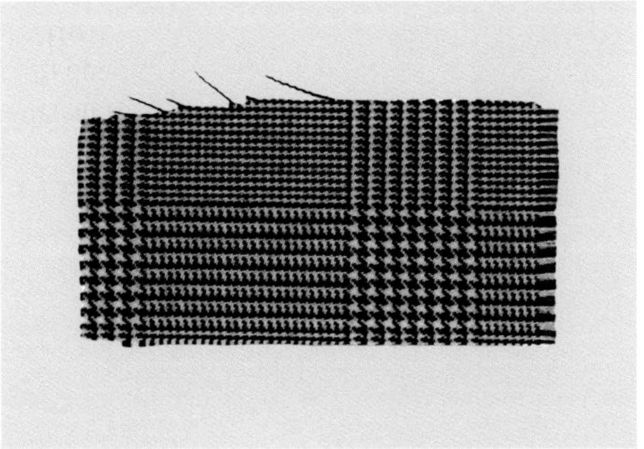

Place d'Youville

Located in Old Montréal, the four-block-long street, Place d'Youville (1997–2002), is set within one of the oldest settlements in western Montréal. Named after Marguerite d'Youville (1701–1771), a founder of the Grey Nuns of Montréal, Place d'Youville was once the location of the Saint Pierre (Peter) River near its confluence with the Saint Lawrence River.[37] In a map dating from 1758, the river can be seen running between the fortifications of the city and the hospital [150].[38] During the early nineteenth century, small bridges spanned the river. They were removed later in the century when the river was diverted into a four-meter-wide underground culvert with the land above it paved. While the site's history eventually faded from public memory, it was precisely this history that Cormier sought to evoke in his design for the area.

By the late 1990s, Place d'Youville was in ruinous condition and bordered by a cacophony of buildings.[39] As Lucie K. Morisset notes, "Taken as a whole, the area appears to be a residual setting, lacking any specific vocation, overlooked by recent restoration efforts in Old Montréal. The challenge then, was to redevelop and unify this clearly important and historically significant site, and especially to imbue it with a fitting identity."[40] When the competition to revive this 3.7-acre space was announced, Cormier invited historians Lucie K. Morisset and Luc Noppen to join his team for the proposal entry, which they won in 1997. To respect and protect the site's archeological history, they capped its center with a concrete slab to prevent the destruction of history buried beneath.[41] Once again, Cormier explored a surface treatment

34 Cormier, interview with Herrington, 25 July 2018.

35 Sven Raphael Schneider, "Bottom Button Rules for Vest & Waistcoat," 4 May 2010, *Gentleman's Gazette*, https://www.gentlemansgazette.com/waiscoat-button/.

36 Cormier, interview with Herrington, 25 July 2018.

37 Lucie K. Morisset, "Of History and Memory: An Allegory of Identity in the Redevelopment of Place d'Youville (Montréal)," *Journal of the Society for the Study of Architecture in Canada* 25, nos. 2–4 (2000), p. 17.

38 R. D. Wilson and Eric McLean, *Montréal*, Montréal: McGill University Press, 1964, n.p. The parking lot on Place d'Youville between rue Saint-Pierre and rue McGill once housed the colonial parliament building.

39 These included former warehouses, the 1992 Museum of Archaeology and History, the stately harbor-related structures from the turn of the century, the 200-year-old buildings once owned by the Grey Nuns, and a fire station dating to 1903 (now a visitor center). See Joshua Wolfe and Cécile Grenier, *Montréal Guide: An Architectural and Historical Guide*, Montréal: Libre Expression, 1983, p. 56.

40 Morisset, "Of History and Memory," p. 17.

41 Another historically relevant event was the fire in 1849. English-speaking Tories, outraged by Lord Elgin's Rebellion Losses Bill, attacked the building, set it on fire at all four corners, and prevented firemen from putting out the fire. The Legislative Council and Assembly never returned to Montréal and eventually a new Parliament building was located in Ottawa.

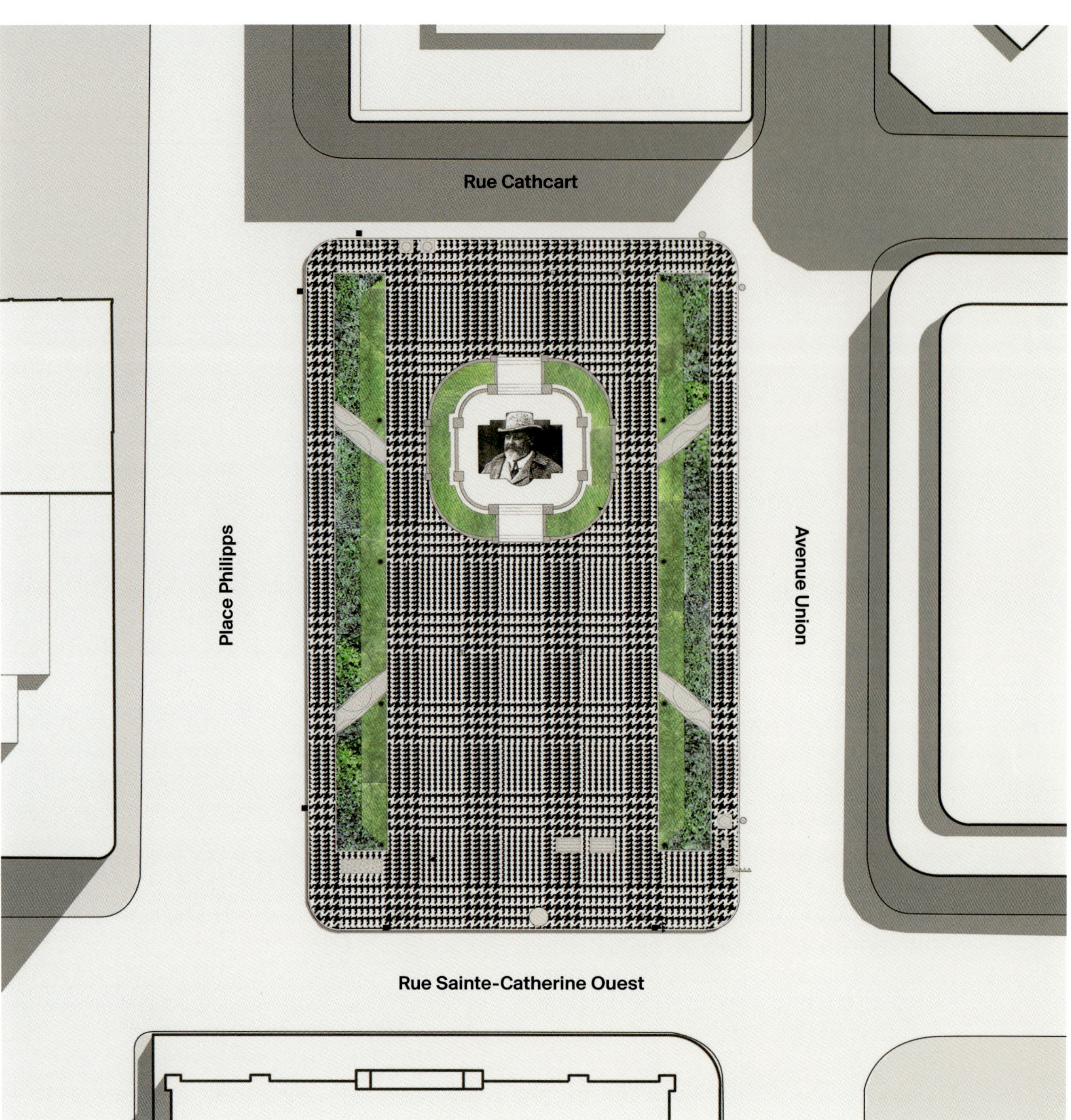
Rue Cathcart
Place Philipps
Avenue Union
Rue Sainte-Catherine Ouest

148
(opposite)
Phillips Square.
Montréal, Québec, 1996.
Conceptual plan.
[Claude Cormier
et Associés]

149
Le Château Apartments.
Montréal, Québec, 2013.
Houndstooth paving
installed.
[Guillaume Paradis, Claude
Cormier et Associés]

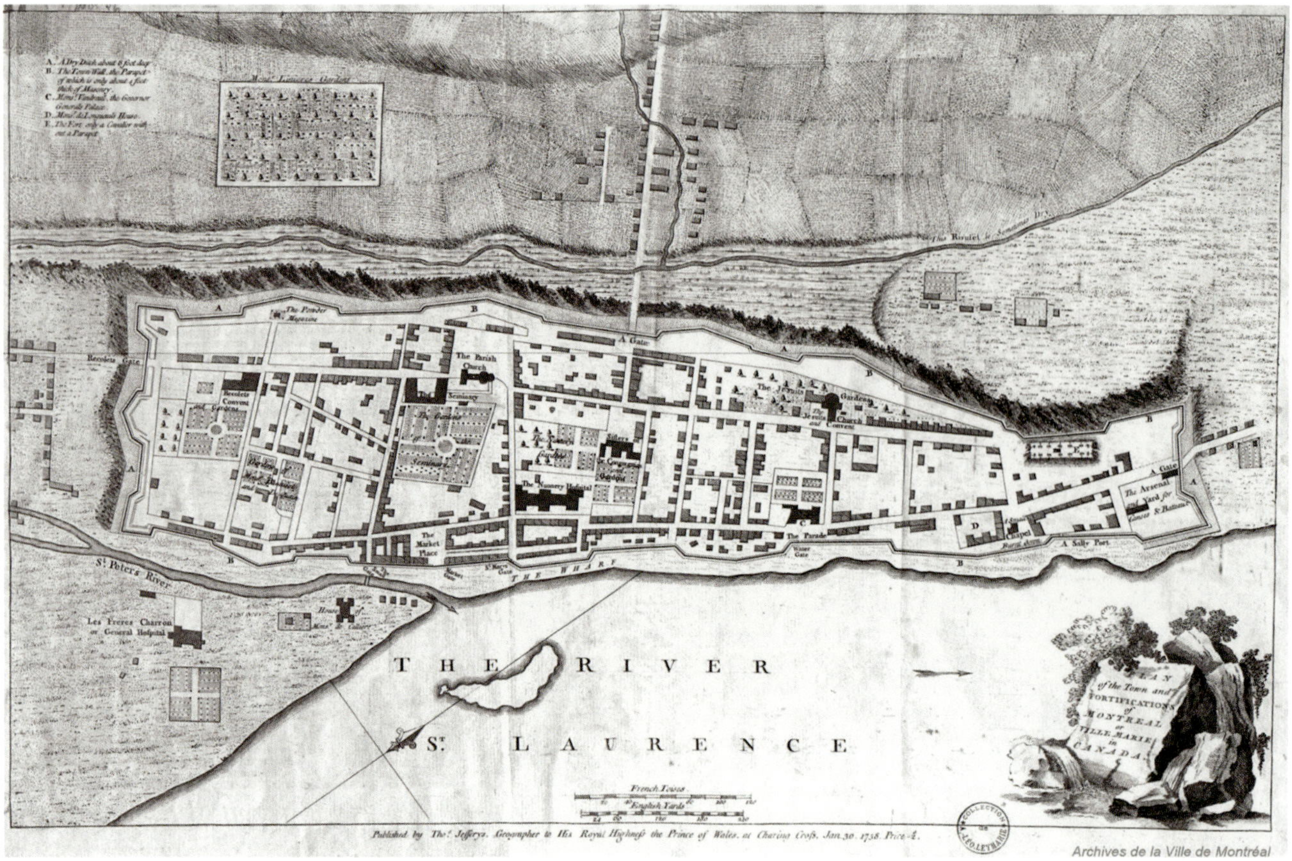
THE RIVER
ST. LAURENCE
The Parish Church
The Market Place
The Parade
A Gate
A Sally Port
St. Peters River
Les Freres Charron or General Hospital
PLAN of the Town and FORTIFICATIONS of MONTREAL or VILLE MARIE in CANADA.
French Toises
English Yards
Published by Thos. Jefferys, Geographer to His Royal Highness the Prince of Wales, at Charing Cross. Jan. 30. 1758. Price 1s.
Archives de la Ville de Montréal

PLACE D'YOUVILLE, CONCEPT URBAIN
FÉVRIER 1997
NO SCALE

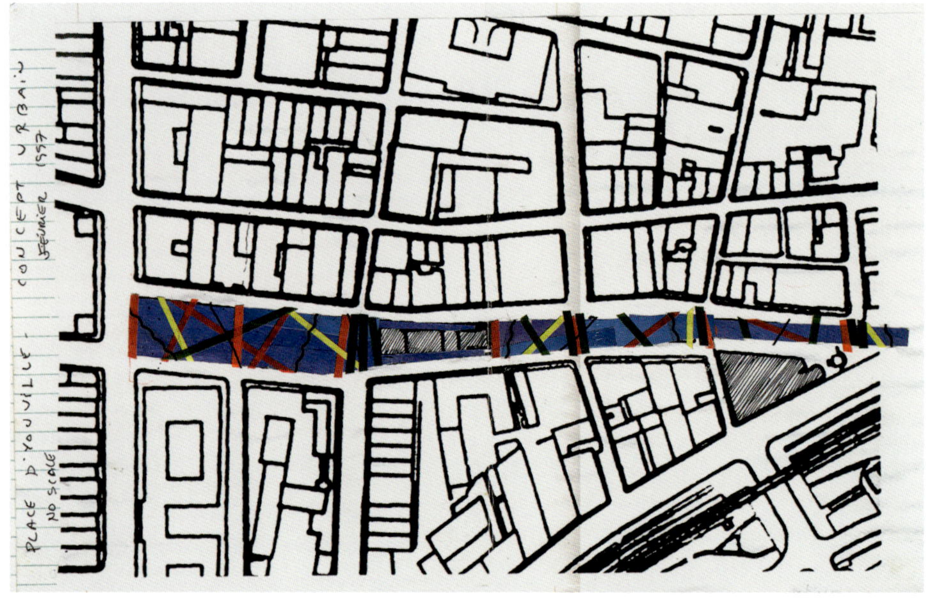

150
(opposite above)
Plan of the town and fortifications of Montréal. Montréal, Québec, 1758. Notice the small river at the lower left-hand side. [Archives de la Ville de Montréal, Public domain]

151
(opposite below)
Place d'Youville. Montréal, Québec, 1997. Conceptual plan. [Canadian Centre for Architecture © Claude Cormier et Associés]

152
Place d'Youville. Montréal, Québec, 2008. Aerial view in fall. [Jean-François Vézina]

to express the site's past. To help unify the site from north to south, Cormier designed a series of pathways that crisscrossed the grass boulevard and connected the doorways of buildings across the way. The paths overlap and create a tapestry of hardscape and grassy wedges [151]. The paths also signal the status of the surrounding historical structures and the diversity of entryways along the Place d'Youville. The materials of the paths, which Cormier has referred to as a long history "of sidewalk construction in the city," express the varied nature of the buildings that flank both sides of the boulevard.[42] Wood was used for paths connecting residential structures, while more enduring materials, such as granite and limestone, linked official structures.

To unify the east–west axis and match the flow of the original river, a wide path of granite pavers runs down the center of the grassed median. With this clever and unobtrusive treatment of the ground plane, Cormier expressed the historic qualities of the site, while offering a visually compelling and useful urban landscape. The entire three-block-long space is bordered by an allée of honey locust trees (*Gleditsia triacanthos inermis*) that further enhances the spatial unification of the site [152].Today, the trees have matured beautifully. Although it's unknown if people ever interpreted the rationale behind the different paving materials, this decision to make the paths resemble a crazy quilt grants these traditional paving materials a new attitude. Moreover, Cormier's use of the paving materials to express the status of the different buildings lining Place d'Youville represents one of his early attempts to bring beauty through meaning to a historic landscape.

Place d'Armes

The origins of the Place d'Armes can be traced back to the very founding of Montréal. In the 1650s the site was used as a cemetery for the Hôtel-Dieu hospital. Some twenty years later it was placed under the aegis of the Sulpicians, a society of diocesan priests, who began constructing Montréal's first Notre-Dame Church, and who in 1693 designated the area to the northwest of the church as a public market called Place de la Fabrique.[43] This first Notre-Dame Church was the brainchild of François Dollier de Casson, a cavalry captain, priest, military chaplain, avid explorer, and superior of the Sulpicians in New France. To enhance its status, Dollier positioned the church in the middle of the newly developed Notre-Dame Street, one of the city's first ten streets.[44] This location in the center of the street was typical of French Catholic churches in Montréal and a sign of their influence in constructing the city's urban fabric. This historical fact would also pique Cormier's imagination when he proposed a design for the site over 300 years later [153].

In 1721 Place de la Fabrique became the primary stage for military drills and was renamed Place d'Armes. During the late eighteenth century and well into the nineteenth century, Place d'Armes was the site of numerous political incidents. During the American occupation of Montréal, for example, the head of the statue of King George III, which sat at the center of the square, was completely

42 Claude Cormier, "Place d'Youville, Montréal (Québec), Canada," Claude Cormier et Associés: Landscape Architecture and Urban Design, http://www.claudecormier.com/en/projet/place-dyouville/.

43 "Place d'Armes," Répertoire du patrimoine culturel du Québec, Québec Culture et Communications, http://www.patrimoine-culturel.gouv.qc.ca/rpcq/detail.do? methode=consulter&id=100097&type=bien#.Wz_PyiOZNgc.

44 Jean-Claude Marsan, *Montreal in Evolution: Historical Analysis of Montreal's Architecture and Urban Environment*, Montréal: McGill-Queen's University Press, 1981, pp. 74–75.

153
Montréal, Québec, 1704.
Plan.
Note the church in the
center of the street
in red (upper area of map).
[Public domain,
United States]

severed, and later found in a well.[45] In 1836 the city of Montréal purchased the land and by the 1850s the square had evolved into a more Anglicized version of urbanism.[46] It was planted with trees and grass, and graced at its center by a statue of Montréal's founding father, Paul Chomedey de Maisonneuve. Much in keeping with squares in London, a wrought-iron fence enclosed its perimeter [154]. Under the new owners, Place d'Armes was also enlarged to measure 344 feet by 392 feet—which roughly corresponds with its current size.[47] Like the square, the new church too was Anglicized. Historians have noted that the new Notre-Dame Church (1829) was constructed in a manner decidedly "influenced by the Gothic Revival as expressed in England."[48] The new church was located adjacent to the old Notre-Dame Church on the edge of Notre-Dame Street. Poignantly, both churches stood side by side for a year [155]. By the start of World War I, the fencing and gardens had been removed from the square and its surface repaved with concrete and stone.

During the twentieth century, Place d'Armes lost its identity as the city's political and financial focal point as the area evolved into a transportation hub and leisure area for tourists. The nineteenth-century buildings surrounding the square, such as the Bank of Montreal building (1847) and the New York Life Insurance Building (1887) helped frame Place d'Armes and lend prominence to the new Notre-Dame Church [156]. However, twentieth-century skyscrapers built around the square, particularly the Aldred Building (1931) and the Banque Canadienne Nationale (1968), towered over it and dwarfed its size.[49]

In October 2007, Claude Cormier et Associés was invited, with three other multidisciplinary teams, to develop proposals for the redevelopment of Place d'Armes. The three teams were also asked to respond to the exhibition *C'est ma place (publique)!* that celebrated visions for the square's future generated by citizens in a workshop-style format. Once again Cormier considered the surface conditions of the square as a source of historical reference.[50] Embracing Place d'Armes' existence as a hard-surfaced urban space and its Francophone heritage (rather than its life as a nineteenth-century English square), Cormier's team proposed to resurface the majority of the site with a mix of cobblestones recovered from Old Montréal, the granite pavers of the 1960s Place d'Armes, and new stones. The low walls constructed around the square in the 1960s were to be removed and the pavers were to extend over the surrounding streets to the building façades—strengthening the visual connection between the buildings and the square. For Cormier, the granite expressed the memory of Place d'Armes as

154
Place d'Armes.
Montréal, Québec, 1876.
As an English square.
[Notman & Sandham,
Musée McCord, II-41752]

155
Robert Auchmuty Sproule. *The Place d'Armes, Montreal, QC, 1828.* Note the two churches stand side by side. [Musée McCord, M385]

it was before the demolition of the original. He even wanted to bring the original church back—well, sort of. Lighter-colored pavers were used to trace the footprint of the first Notre-Dame Church—highlighting the French tradition of placing the church in the middle of the street [157].

Cormier had originally sought to raise the church footprint to the height of a speed bump that would also serve as a drop-off area for the church, which had been the setting for numerous high-profile weddings, such as Celine Dion's marriage to René Angélil.[51] The idea was rejected by the Ministry of Culture, however. Additionally, Cormier's proposal called for an illuminated cross to be suspended in the air over Notre-Dame Street (approximately where the cross had capped the steeple of the old Notre-Dame Church); not surprisingly, this idea was rejected too [158].[52] Today, this reference to the old church is most striking viewed from Google Earth, although, looking down from one of the surrounding skyscrapers might afford more prominent views of the footprint of the demolished church.

Claude Cormier et Associés also proposed accommodating the square's current use as a leisure area, with allées of trees on its northwest and southeast sides. They also envisioned unabashedly contemporary lighting and seating that markedly contrasted with the historical paving and the Maisonneuve statue and fountain. During a visit on a warm July afternoon, throngs of people were moving through the square, while others sat on the benches that line its sides. The low seating platforms were particularly popular with people lounging in different positions, some lying down as if on a beach, others with crossed legs sitting in small groups. Unfortunately, Cormier and his team were never given credit for the redesign of Place d'Armes [159]. The executed design was based on ideas created during the workshop in 2007. If you view the design proposals online today, you will see it was the

45 For example, in 1760 the Place d'Armes was the repository of French muskets surrendered to the British Army. Three years after the French colony was made a British possession, a bust of George III of Britain was erected in the center of Place d'Armes. In 1774 the bust was vandalized in reaction to the Quebec Act, which gave new privileges to French Canadians. Protesters hung a potato rosary around the king's neck with a cross on it that read, "Behold, the Pope of Canada, or the English idiot." See "Place d'Armes: Old Montreal's Public Square Cradle of City's Long History," *The Guardian*, 22 November 2011, http://www.theguardian.pe.ca/living/place-darmes-old-Montréals-public-square-cradle-of-citys-long-history-108901/.

46 Wolfe and Grenier, *Montréal Guide*, p. 78.

47 Marsan, *Montréal in Evolution*, p. 141.

48 Ibid., p. 74.

49 Ibid., p. 75.

50 Cormier, interview with Herrington, 25 July 2018.

51 Conversation, Cormier, Parent, Treib, and Herrington, 9 July 2017, Place d'Armes, Montréal.

52 Ibid.

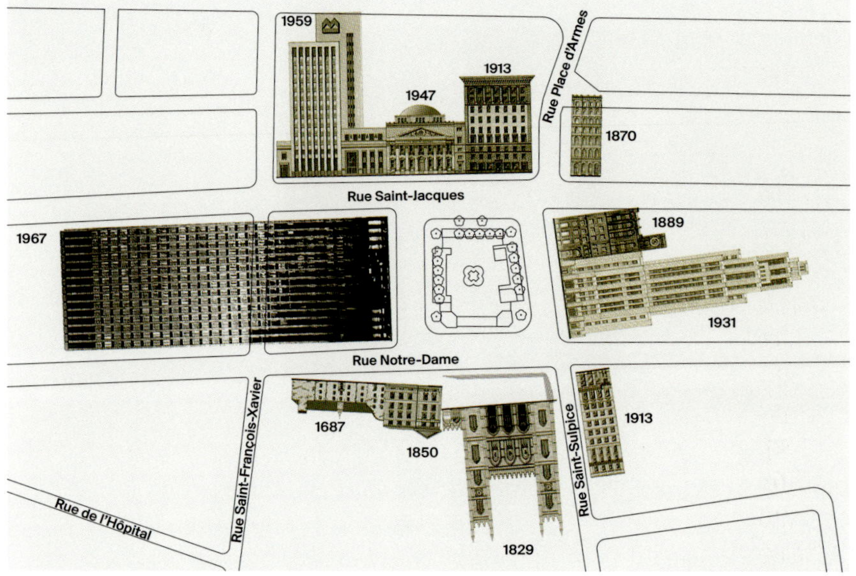

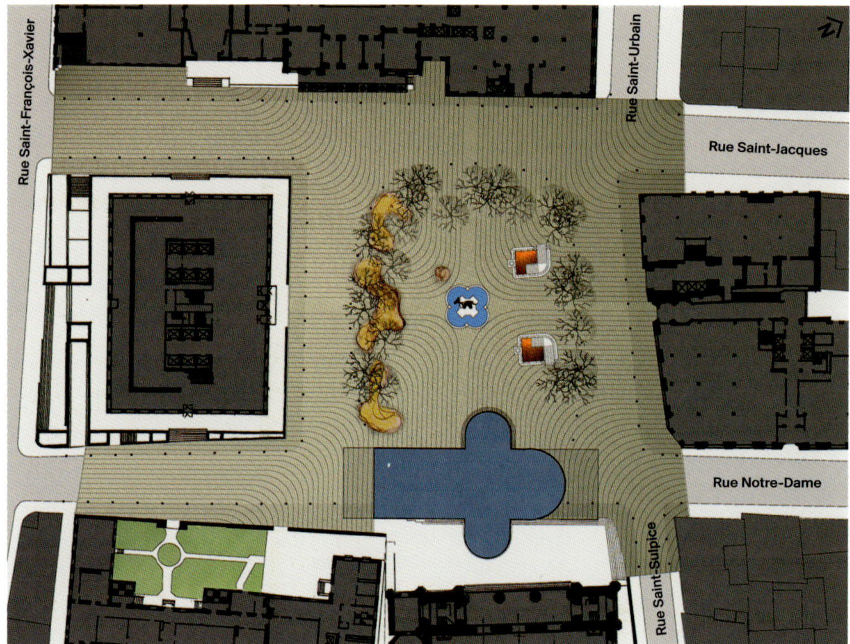

156
Place d'Armes.
Montréal, Québec, 2007.
Context collage.
[Claude Cormier
et Associés]

157
Place d'Armes.
Conceptual plan.
[Claude Cormier
et Associés]

158
(opposite above)
Place d'Armes.
Proposed suspended cross.
[Claude Cormier
et Associés]

159
(opposite below)
Place d'Armes.
Montréal, Québec, 2011.
Project as built by Lemay
(formerly Groupe Cardinal
Hardy) and the City of
Montréal.
[Bernard Lewy Bertaut]

ideas put forth by Claude Cormier et Associés that were primarily built.[53] Nonetheless, at the time Cormier was also working on the renovations to Dorchester Square, where his design ideas were steadily being acknowledged and realized.

Dorchester Square and Place du Canada

Located in the commercial center of downtown Montréal, the Dorchester Square and Place du Canada projects demanded the most rigorous historical research by the firm to date. Cormier's office coproduced the master plan's first phase with Lemay (formerly Groupe Cardinal Hardy) and the City of Montréal, and working with the landscape architect Jonathan Cha, they also helped the City of Montréal's strategic plan and archival research for the area. In 2010, Claude Cormier et Associés published *Réaménagement et mise en valeur du square Dorchester et de la place du Canada*, a 115-page historical analysis of the site and plans for its renovation.[54]

Their historical research about the area revealed that during the early nineteenth century it had been the Saint-Antoine Catholic Cemetery, which primarily served poor Irish families and provided inspiration for Cormier. With the cholera epidemic of 1832, thousands of victims who had died from the infectious disease were interred at Saint-Antoine Cemetery and it began to reach capacity. The neighborhood surrounding the cemetery was also evolving into the "new" downtown as people began migrating from what is now called Old Montréal, exacerbating developmental pressures.[55] The cemetery was closed in 1854 and the land was sold to a developer who began exhuming graves and relocating them to Notre-Dame-des-Neiges Cemetery on Mount Royal. With the advice of the Montreal Sanitary Association and a supporting petition signed by local residents, the movement of bodies from the cemetery halted and thousands still lie below the site today.[56] This lesser-known history of the site would later inspire Cormier in his renovation of Dorchester Square.

The city expropriated the four-acre site in 1870 with plans to convert the former cemetery into a public space so as not to disturb the graves.[57] It was named Dominion Square in honor of the newly formed Dominion of Canada.[58] Dorchester Boulevard (today the busy René-Lévesque Boulevard) divides the two sites. Aerial views reveal that the two sites are not aligned but are staggered east to west, reflecting the shape of the site when it was a cemetery. While the north side's layout is fully committed to the symmetrical order found in French gardens, the square to the south is more reminiscent of a picturesque park [160]. The urban edges of the two sites differ as well. Surrounding the north side of the square, banks and insurance company buildings hug the edges of the sidewalks,[59] while to the south, the site is surrounded by two churches and other structures set back into grassy parcels of land. It is unknown if the use of these two

53 Jennifer Edwards, "Place d'Armes," *Infopresse*, 1 November 2007, https://www.infopresse.com/archive/article/24255.

54 Claude Cormier Architectes Paysagistes Inc., Groupe Cardinal Hardy, and Teknika-HBA, *Réaménagement et mise en valeur du square Dorchester et de la place du Canada*, June 2009.

55 Wolfe and Grenier, *Montréal Guide*, pp. 94–95.

56 This activity enraged people because not only was it deemed sacrilegious, but also there was worry that workers removing the bodies of cholera victims would expose themselves to the disease.

57 Wolfe and Grenier, *Montréal Guide*, pp. 94–95.

58 The plans devised for the square have been attributed to the City of Montréal surveyor Patrick Macquisten, who developed a plan entitled, "Proposed Improvement of the Roman Catholic Burying Ground." The south side was completed in 1876, while the northern portion opened in 1882. Email exchange with Ron Williams, 24 August 2018.

59 Conversation, Cormier, Parent, Treib, and Herrington, 9 July 2017, Dorchester Square, Montréal.

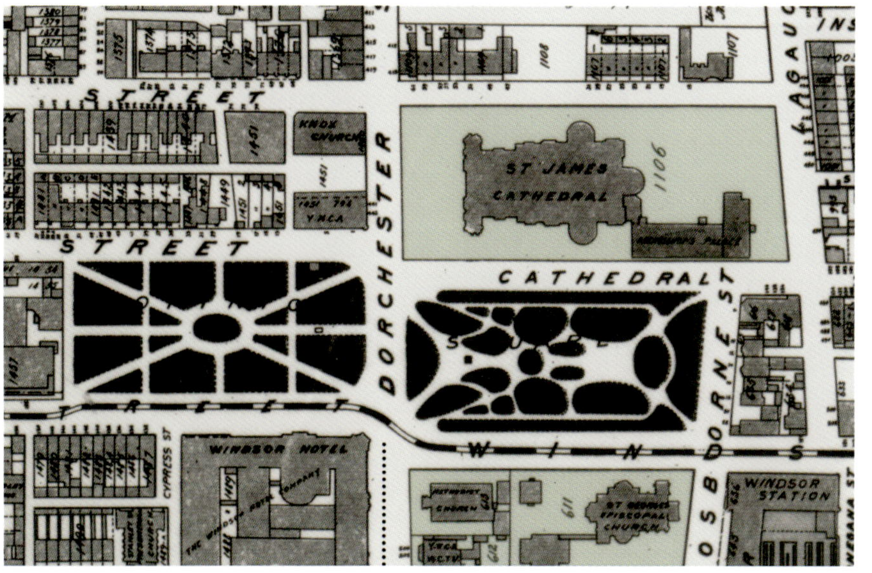

160
Dominion Square,
Montréal, Québec, 1907.
Plan showing formal
and more organic layouts
for the different sites.
[*Pinsonneault Atlas*. Detail
National Archives of
Canada, Ottawa, NMC-16305]

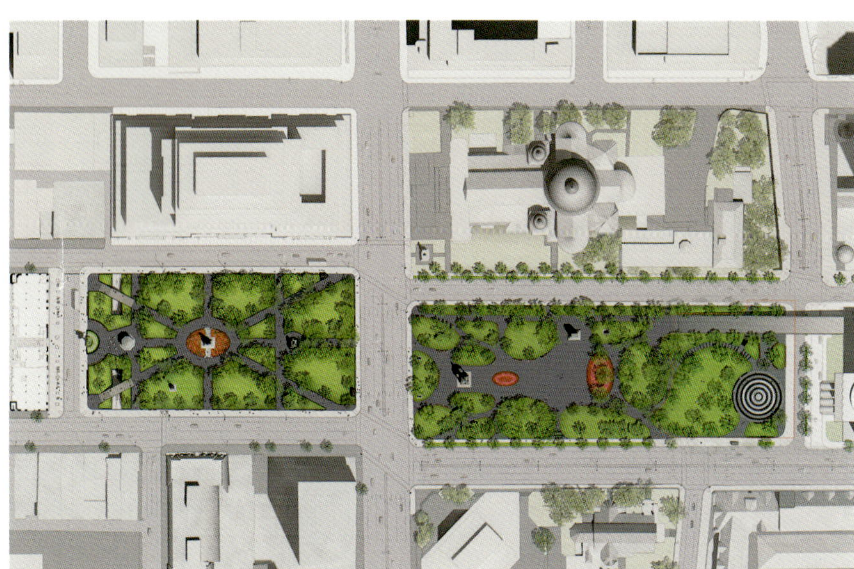

161
Dorchester Square
and Place du Canada.
Montréal, Québec, 2008.
Plan.
[Claude Cormier
et Associés]

162
Dorchester Square.
New trees, paving,
and benches.
[Raphaël Thibodeau]

different styles, English and French, was intentional or created as a celebration of the duality of languages spoken in Montreal. Nonetheless, it's a uniquely Montréal urban expression and one seen in the city's historic architecture as well. In 1966 to celebrate the World's Fair, Expo 67, the south side of Dominion Square was renamed Place du Canada and in 1988 the north side of Dominion Square was renamed Dorchester Square, after Guy Carleton, 1st Baron of Dorchester. Ironically, while Dominion Square had been named to symbolize the unification of Canada, the square's union did not survive the twentieth century.

Over the years, however, architecturally distinguished buildings were constructed around Dorchester Square and Place du Canada.[60] And like many urban landscapes, both sites had become repositories for numerous commemorative statues and plaques attesting to the country's official history.[61] When Claude Cormier et Associés was commissioned to renovate the two sites, much of the nineteenth-century design work had already been destroyed. At Dorchester Square, two ramps leading to an underground parking garage had been constructed, interrupting the diagonal paths leading to the central Boer War Memorial statue. The basic layout of pathways in both squares had been completely obliterated. The Norway maples (*Acer platanoides*) planted decades ago had grown considerably, obstructing views of the architecturally rich surrounds. Moreover, this type of maple is notorious for creating deep shade, and with little access to sunlight, the grassy areas turned into mud. In response to this dismal condition, the city installed asphalt pathways and picnic benches in the muddy expanses.

After carefully researching the site's history, Cormier reinstated the formal layout of paths in Dorchester Square and the looser, English-inspired pathway vocabulary of Place du Canada [161]. At Dorchester Square he improved upon the existing design by creating gently sloping grass mounds that give spatial definition to the pathways and provide a dry place to sit. Granite curbs, twice the width of regular curbing, support these mounds and emphasize the elegant lines of the paths [162]. Cormier also paid special attention to the seating at Dorchester Square. The oak benches were grouped together in pairs and, where they appear at the central circular area, they have been shaped to match the curvature of the granite curbing. The new pathways are surfaced with a mix of three types of granite pavers, each with a different finish [163] [164]. The new granite paving produces a shimmering effect, especially at night with the new lighting scheme, but also in the dappled light produced by another major improvement Cormier made to Dorchester Square—new trees. Cormier replaced the Norway maples with a mix of sugar maples (*Acer saccharum*), silver maples (*Acer saccharinum* "Silver Queen"), Freeman's maples (*Acer x freemanii*), red maples (*Acer rubrum*), and elms (*Ulmus accolade*). The subtle mixture of these tree types, which do not create the deep shade produced by Norway maples, has enabled the grass to thrive. Sadly, many of the refined details of Dorchester Square are absent from Place du Canada. The south side has no curbing or low mounds, and the benches are placed randomly and do not follow the lines of the paths. This is due to the fact that Claude Cormier et Associés

60 These buildings include Mary Queen of the World Cathedral (1894), a miniature replica of St. Peter's in Rome, Windsor Station (1900–1950), the Sun Life Building (1914), which was the largest building in Canada at the time, and the two-faced façades of the Dominion Square Building (1927). See Wolfe and Grenier, *Montréal Guide*, p. 95.

61 Some of these include a tribute to Sir Wilfrid Laurier (1953), Canada's first French-Canadian prime minister, the Boer War Memorial (1907) (also known as Strathcona's Horse), and the Montréal Cenotaph (1921). See Ron Williams, *Landscape Architecture in Canada*, McGill-Queen's University Press, 2014, for a discussion on Dorchester Square, p. 159.

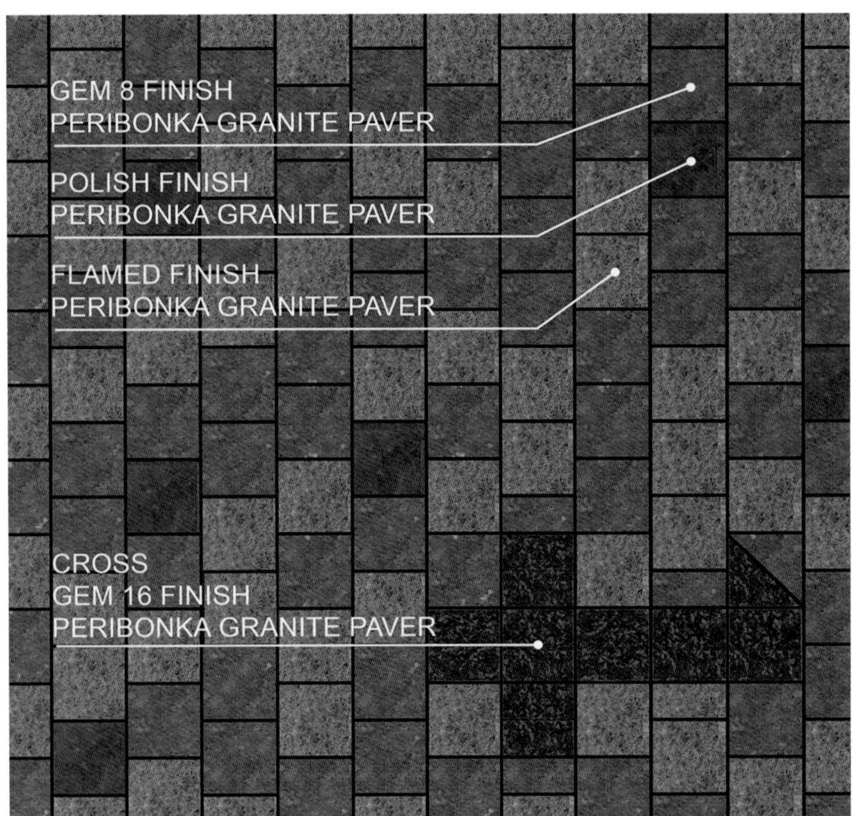

163
Dorchester Square.
Montréal, Québec, 2010.
Granite paving types.
[Claude Cormier
et Associés]

164
(opposite)
Dorchester Square.
New lighting scheme.
[Marc Cramer]

IMAX

165
Dorchester Square and Place du Canada. Montréal, Québec, 2008. Overlay of St-Antoine Cemetery with current site. [Claude Cormier et Associés]

166
(opposite)
Dorchester Square, North Portion. Montréal, Québec, 2019. New bridges serve as informal seating areas. [Raphaël Thibodeau]

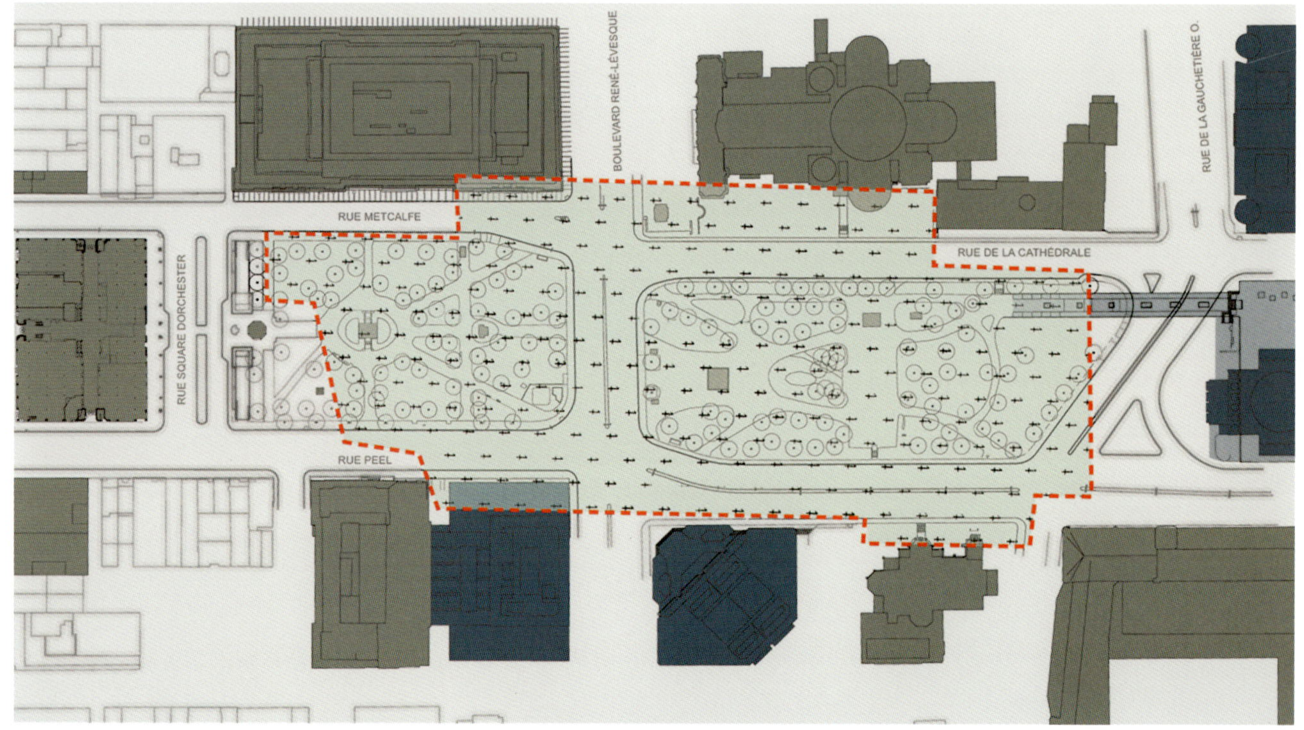

Infotouriste
simons

167
Karl Blossfeldt.
Urformen der Kunst.
Horsetail
(*Equisetum hyemale*), 1928.
[Public domain, United States]

did not complete Place du Canada's construction documents and construction observations.[62]

Despite the plethora of official historical narratives displayed above ground in the statues and plaques at Dorchester Square and Place du Canada, Claude Cormier et Associés sought to underscore the site's buried history—60,000 graves that Cormier discovered in archival maps of Saint-Antoine Catholic Cemetery [165]. There is parking and other infrastructure underneath the sites, but there are also bodies beneath the entire area that have never been removed.[63] Similar to how Cormier had treated other historically significant landscapes, he focused on the ground plane as a source of memory and expression. To subtly reference the Catholic people buried below, Cormier embedded rough-cut black granite pavers with cross symbols, each with its own coordinate, flush with the paving surface. Cormier's cross signs originate from the cartographic symbols indicating the presence of a cemetery.

In 2019, Claude Cormier and company completed the northern parcel of Dorchester Square. Cormier reestablished the geometrical pattern of the original design installed in the nineteenth century with two arched pedestrian bridges that cross over the underground parkade egress lanes. The bridges not only restore the historical axes but they also provide easier access for pedestrians coming from the busy Sainte-Catherine Street area to the north [166].[64]

Cormier's ornamental water feature was inspired by the 1875 fountain at Viger Square in Montréal. Cormier transformed the fountain for Dorchester Square by replacing the statuettes and urns in the Viger Square fountain with a giant reedlike stalk of a rough horsetail (*Equisetum hyemale*) cast in aluminum. The stalk imagery was borrowed from black and white photographs of a horsetail plant taken by photographer Karl Blossfeldt, who had a knack for making the pliable stems, stalks, and leaves of plant material look as if they had been cast in metal [167] [168].[65] Cormier sliced the fountain due to spatial and structural restraints [169] [170], but the idea of slicing the fountain was inspired by his artist friend Georges Audet who regularly slices figurines of the holy family [171].

62 Conversation, Cormier, Parent, Treib, and Herrington, 9 July 2017, Dorchester Square, Montréal.

63 In fact, in 2009 and 2011, during the renovations of Dorchester Square, workers encountered fifteen bodies, some buried only fourteen inches below the paving. See Catherine Solyom, "Skeletal Remains Open Window to Our Past," *Montreal Gazette*, 9 October 2009, https://www.pressreader.com/canada/Montréal-gazette/20091009/281586646653149.

64 Andy Riga, "Dorchester Square to Get a Victorian Fountain in Renovation Project," *Montreal Gazette*, 23 May 2018, https://Montréalgazette.com/news/local-news/dorchester-square-to-get-a-victorian-fountain-in-renovation-project.

65 See Karl Blossfeldt, *Urformen der Kunst* (Art Forms in Nature: Enlarged Photographs of Plant Forms), New York: Universe Books, 1967.

168
Dorchester Square,
North Portion.
Montréal, Québec, 2019.
View of new fountain.
[Jean Blais]

169
(overleaf)
Dorchester Square,
North Portion.
The sliced fountain
seen from the rear.
[Jean-François Savaria]

170
(Opposite)
Dorchester Square,
North Portion.
Montréal, Québec, 2019.
The sliced fountain
and woodpecker.
[Raphaël Thibodeau]

171
Georges Audet.
Sliced Holy Family.
Montréal, Québec, 2003.
Inspiration for sliced
fountain.
[Georges Audet]

National Holocaust Monument

Prior to the National Holocaust Monument project (2017) in Ottawa, many of Cormier's Montréal heritage landscapes were informed by the history of the city. The Holocaust Monument forced Cormier to grapple with a history significantly graver. The project is also one of the few instances where plant life becomes the primary material of expression and meaning. In many of the firm's projects, plant life, particularly trees, is carefully handled to frame space and provide shade. For the National Holocaust Monument, however, trees would play a primary role in expressing the resilience of Jews who fled to Canada to rebuild their lives.

The multidisciplinary team comprised Studio Daniel Libeskind, Edward Burtynsky, and Doris Bergen, and was assembled by Lord Cultural Resources. Libeskind and Cormier had worked previously together on the Sony Centre for the Performing Arts in Toronto, where Cormier had designed the entry plaza in conjunction with the renovation of the performance center and new residential tower designed by Libeskind. There, Cormier's plaza took its cues from the acute angles of the architecture with an Escher-like geometric paving pattern of black and white granite. The illusionary qualities of this pattern are dizzyingly magnified in the reflective surfaces of Harley Valentine's twisting, mirrored sculptures, entitled *Dream Ballet* [172].

Cormier was impressed with Libeskind's positive energy on the Sony project; however, when Libeskind asked him to join the competition team, Cormier at first declined.[66] As it happens he had already been invited by several other architects to participate, but he demurred, finding the subject too psychologically heavy. More importantly, Cormier was not a Jew and he felt his participation would be inappropriate.[67] Libeskind persisted and assured Cormier that their submission would be about hope and survival, and Cormier acquiesced.

Of the seventy-two professional teams that entered the competition, a shortlist whittled this number down to six, and the team's scheme, entitled "Landscape of Loss, Memory and Survival," was awarded first place and the commission. The monument sought to memorialize not only the Holocaust victims but also the surviving 40,000 Jews who fled to Canada after the war and remained here. The project's goal was to "strike a balance between the Holocaust's universal significance and the Canadian context. This balance had to be expressed through the spaces of the monument, its relationship to the adjacent Canadian War Museum, the vistas toward Parliament Hill, the materials, the architecture, the landscape and the art."[68]

Canada's historical relationship with the Holocaust, its survivors, and its victims is problematic at best.[69] The Canadian government's censorship of the news regarding the Holocaust and the plight of Jews in Europe, coupled with widespread anti-Semitism resulted in restrictions placed on Jewish migration.[70] By the start of the

66 Cormier and Parent, interview with Treib and Herrington, 9 July 2017, Montréal.

67 Cormier, interview with Herrington, 21 June 2018.

68 Gail Dexter Lord and Dov Goldstein, "Our Journey Toward Canada's Holocaust Monument: Personal Reflection by Gail Dexter Lord and Dov Goldstein," Lord Cultural Resources, 2017, p. 3.

69 Despite the efforts of the Canadian Jewish Congress and the Jewish Labour Committee, "the Canadian government lacked the political will to rescue Jewish refugees who had been smuggled out of Hitler's empire during the war." See Norman Erwin, "The Holocaust, Canadian Jews, and Canada's 'Good War' against Nazism," *Canadian Jewish Studies / Études juives canadiennes* 24, 2016, p. 118.

70 Canada accepted only 5,000 Jewish immigrants (compared to 200,000 Jews who entered the United States) during World War II. See Aaron Beswick, "Canada Turned Away Jewish Refugees," 15 December 2013, http://thechronicleherald.ca/novascotia/1174272-canada-turned-away-jewish-refugees.

172
Studio Daniel Libeskind with Claude Cormier et Associés, Page + Steele / IBI Group Architects, and Harley Valentine (public art).
Sony Centre for the Performing Arts.
Toronto, Ontario, 2015.
View of paving with *Harley Valentine's Dream Ballet*.
[Industryous Photography]

173
Studio Daniel Libeskind in collaboration with Claude Cormier et Associés, Edward Burtynsky, and Doris Bergen.
National Holocaust Monument.
Ottawa, Ontario, 2017.
[Doublespace Photography]

174
Studio Daniel Libeskind with Claude Cormier et Associés, Edward Burtynsky, and Doris Bergen.
National Holocaust Monument.
Ottawa, Ontario, 2017.
[Studio Libeskind]

175
(opposite)
Studio Daniel Libeskind with Claude Cormier et Associés, Edward Burtynsky, and Doris Bergen.
National Holocaust Monument.
Entrance ramp.
[Doublespace Photography]

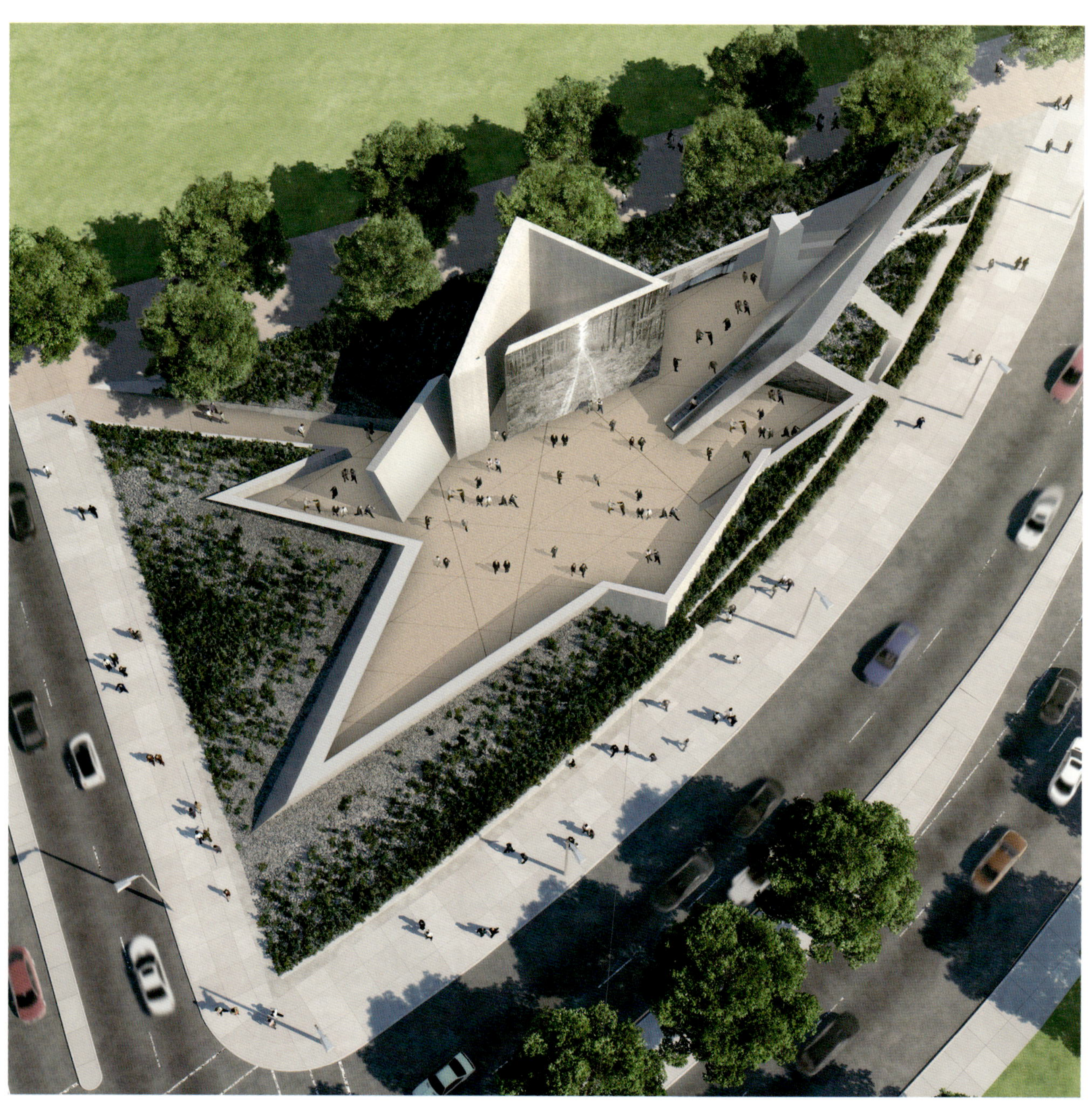

NATIONAL HOLOCAUST MONUMENT
MONUMENT NATIONAL DE L'HOLOCAUSTE

176
Studio Daniel Libeskind with Claude Cormier et Associés, Edward Burtynsky, and Doris Bergen.
National Holocaust Monument.
Ottawa, Ontario, 2017.
Reproduced photographs by Edward Burtynsky.
[Doublespace Photography]

177
(page 229)
Studio Daniel Libeskind with Claude Cormier et Associés, Edward Burtynsky, and Doris Bergen.
National Holocaust Monument.
View through Stairs of Hope to Parliament.
[Doublespace Photography]

twenty-first century, Ottawa was the only capital city of the Allied nations without a Holocaust memorial. This fact incensed an eighteen-year-old granddaughter of a Holocaust survivor, Laura Grosman, who sparked the campaign to create a monument.[71] In 2012 the Canadian government announced the formation of the National Holocaust Monument Development Council whose charge was to raise funds to cover the cost of the design, construction, and maintenance of the memorial. The one-acre triangular site assigned to the project sits on the corner of Wellington Street and Booth Street in Ottawa. The site also faces the Canadian War Museum and affords views to the rooftops of Parliament, two details that would significantly guide the team's design and its interpretation of hope [173].

Cost overruns and delays that enabled refinements to the project details prolonged the project by two years, but in the summer of 2017 construction of the National Holocaust Monument was complete. Executed in cast-in-place concrete, the monument's design was derived from an elongated Star of David, the symbol that Jews were forced to wear during the Holocaust [174]. This symbol was manipulated in plan and served to position the slanting contours of the monument's walls, although the star figure is indecipherable when seen from the ground. Poignantly, the entrance is aligned with the Canadian War Museum and a ramp descends at a 5 percent grade through Cormier's landscape and down into the monument [175]. The monument confronts visitors with a series of outdoor rooms and alcove spaces for orientation and entry, contemplation, gathering, and interpretation. Edward Burtynsky's photographs of abandoned concentration camps in Germany, Poland, and Czechoslovakia cover the expanses of the concrete walls [176]. The axis, which aligns with the War Museum, continues through the monument and leads to an angled staircase called the Stairs of Hope that brings people to views of the rooftops of the Parliament Buildings [177].

Cormier's landscape is, of course, the aspect of the monument visitors first encounter. The boreal forests in the tree-line regions of Canada's North served as a metaphor for the struggle and resiliency of the Holocaust survivors and their children in Canada. An apt metaphor, trees in these regions of Canada are short in stature as they struggle to survive the extreme climate and poor soils of the North. Cormier's landscape employed genetically dwarfed trees, such as Mugo pines (*Pinus mugo* 'Mops') [178]. These pine trees grow very slowly and despite being members of the genus *pinus* they will reach only four feet in height.[72] The dwarf tree saplings were laid out in a field of pebbles of varying sizes that mimic the rocky terrain of the high-elevation tree-line zones [179]. Underneath Cormier's landscape is, of course, a healthy soil mix that will ensure the survival of the dwarf forest.

As a symbol of the survivors and their children who strove to overcome the devastating legacy of the Holocaust, this scrubby landscape set around a monument of towering slabs of concrete stands out with a distinct identity—one that demands interpretation. Not only because it is a part of a memorial, but also because it contrasts noticeably with Ottawa's other urban landscapes and gardens. Aside from Cornelia Hahn Oberlander's Taiga Garden at the nearby National Gallery, Ottawa's landscape, like those of many capital cities, is one of picturesque parks and ceremonial lawns with displays of red and white tulips. These are a far cry from Cormier's landscape of rock

71 Andrew Duffy, "How an Ottawa Student's Outrage Led to the National Holocaust Monument," *Ottawa Citizen*, 6 September 2017, https://ottawacitizen.com/news/local-news/how-an-ottawa-students-outrage-led-to-the-national-holocaust-monument.

72 Email correspondence with Georges-Étienne Parent, 18 July 2018.

Subalpine fir
Pacific silver fir
Grand fir
Western red cedar
Alaska yellow cypress
Western Hemlock
Sitka spruce
White/Engelmann spruce
Western larch
Douglas-fir
Lodgepole pine
Western white pine
Ponderosa pine

178
(opposite)
National Holocaust Monument.
Ottawa, Ontario, 2017.
Research on dwarf trees.
[© Province of British Columbia. All rights reserved. Reproduced with permission of the Province of British Columbia]

179
National Holocaust Monument.
Dwarf trees installed.
[Marc Treib]

and stunted trees. Over time, regular visitors to the monument are likely to ask, why haven't the pine trees grown?

Cormier's historically grounded projects are not as well known as his beaches or temporary gardens. They are certainly not standard heritage projects, however, as historical references are always delivered with a new attitude. The outline of the old Notre-Dame church reminds us of the French Catholic practice of building churches in the middle of the street. The material palette of pathways at Place d'Youville captures the diversity of building types that have endured in this very old part of Montréal and the lost Saint Pierre River. The homage to the dead beneath Dorchester Square is not made with Celtic crosses but with the cartographic symbol for graveyards used in contemporary French maps. Indeed, a subtle beauty endures, one that juxtaposes the factual and the imaginary elements of the past in a way that heightens our awareness of our participation in the making of history.

Better Living through Landscape

At home and at work with Claude Cormier

If Cormier's landscapes represent serious fun, his *approach* to design entails serious fun too. With verve and ingenuity in spades, Cormier's dedication to both the conceptual dimension and the technical execution of his work parallels the approach of many artists. Interviewing Cormier, Marc Treib and I asked him if he considered his work art. Not art per se, was Cormier's response, and then he explained:

> *We are creative problem solvers; we need to accommodate peoples' desires and address the demands of the project. We have a design practice, not an art studio, and we never have carte blanche. Yes, we flirt with art in the design process, but first of all, the project must work; it must adhere to the building codes, traffic engineering, design standards, and a thick set of guidelines. Ninety percent of the time we are keeping the conceptual integrity focused and quietly herding people without being difficult... just persistent!*[73]

As a member of Cormier's team noted, "We also treat ecological responsibility as an aspect of the best practices to be implemented. ...We are always pushing to have as many trees as appropriate and to give them exemplary conditions in which to grow. Claude loves to work in a collaborative environment. He sits here," pointing to the brightly lit studio where we are talking, "and sketches and talks to the team. He always leads the team, and he leads us with a clear design intent."[74]

Surely direct leadership of the fourteen people who work in the office has been greatly facilitated by its location and that of Cormier's home, affectionately named Le Château Noir, within the same building. Once the site of a wood-furniture shop, the three-story structure faces the now-defunct Carrières incinerator in the Petite-Patrie neighborhood of Montréal. Cormier asked the artist and architect-designer Jacques Bilodeau to help design the new building. Bilodeau responded with architecture that plays on the idea of landscape, while also creating a home uniquely expressing the personality of its occupant, Claude Cormier. At Le Château Noir there are almost no level horizontal or vertical surfaces (apart from the perimeter wall), and the definition of most of the internal spaces within is only suggested. Throughout the house, walls made from sheet metal or black rubber slant noticeably; some can be opened to reveal a bathroom or spare bedroom. White-painted steel catwalks crisscross overhead and lead to Cormier's personal abode and a rooftop garden. According to Cormier, the goal of the design was to "celebrate discomfort and not jam it full of stuff," clearly a unique design brief.[75] The mirrored ceilings of the bathroom and kitchen heighten this feeling of awareness. He notes, "Jacques taught me that; the notion that being unstable makes you much more aware of your own self. I love my house."[76]

In the kitchen of Le Château Noir, a switch beneath the sink activates a hydraulic lift that opens and closes the ceiling. Opening the kitchen ceiling reveals views to the front door and living room [**180**]. Closed, the domesticity imparted by the kitchen is hidden from view: the top of the ceiling serves as a ramp up to an industrial-sized stainless steel bathtub and the rubber room above [**181**]. This room, cloaked in black rubber, reads like a rubber-lined shelf protruding from the wall. It's just big enough for a double bed and a shelf—and it's quite comfortable. In all, Cormier has kitted out Le Château Noir with a range of features marked by serious fun. The toilets are black and stainless steel, and were designed for use primarily in prisons. The living room is home to a stainless steel couch that is covered with a delightfully soft pink mohair upholstery accompanied by matching pillows and a throw that can be worn over the shoulders, if in the mood [**182**]. Bilodeau designed Cormier a home that not only makes you very aware of your body and your movement, but he has also created a house that in every detail reflects the tastes and values of its owner.

In past years, professional landscape architects and architects were forced to conceal their sexual orientation. For example, Christopher Tunnard attempted to hide his sexual orientation when teaching at Harvard University as did James Rose at that same institution. Cormier is one of the few openly gay landscape architects. But does his sexual orientation influence his design process or the work itself? "No, but maybe yes, in a quiet way," he responded.

> *I am honest about who I am. I've never played someone else. I didn't design pink trees at the Montréal Convention Centre as a gay statement, although it was gutsy. I don't think there is a gay landscape architecture, but when I was starting out, I had a few gay role models who were older than me and they had to fight to be respected. These were people not from landscape architecture, but professionals from banking, law, and accounting. When we presented our work a couple of years ago at Harvard, a young male instructor came up to me after the seminar and said, "Claude, you are such a role model; you are not afraid of saying it, you're not afraid of who you are." This impressed [on] me that I should continue. It's positive reinforcement both ways.*[77]

There may not be a gay landscape architecture, but Cormier came out in the 1980s when heteronormative assumptions prevailed more than they do today—at least in some places. Given Cormier's distinctive use of color, his dedication to unconventional ideas, and the great vitality he brings to the work of Claude Cormier et Associés, he is

73 Cormier and Parent, interview with Treib and Herrington, 9 July 2017.

74 Ibid.

75 Cormier, interview with Herrington, 18 August 2018.

76 Kristina Ljubanovic, "Favourite Room: Landscape Architect Claude Cormier's Montreal Home Is Just What You'd Expect—Playful and Engaging," *The Globe and Mail*, 25 January 2018, https://www.theglobeandmail.com/life/home-and-garden/decor/landscape-architects-Montréal-home/article37729370/.

77 Cormier, interview with Herrington, 6 April 2018.

180
(opposite)
Jacques Bilodeau.
Le Château Noir.
Montréal, Québec, 2013.
The kitchen ceiling open.
[Jacques Perron]

181
Jacques Bilodeau.
Le Château Noir.
The kitchen ceiling
closed.
[Jacques Perron]

182
Jacques Bilodeau.
Le Château Noir.
Montréal, Québec, 2013.
Couch.
[Jacques Perron]

183
U.S. First Lady Jacqueline Kennedy in pink with President John F. Kennedy and French Culture Minister André Malraux. Washington, DC, 1962. [White House photo, Public domain]

undoubtedly the Freddie Mercury of landscape architecture. Not surprisingly, this verve is most evident when he works with design review panels and developers.

Working with Design Review Panels and Developers

According to his team, "In each project Claude likes to challenge the people involved, including the review boards, and in turn they challenge us back."[78] At the design review level, in fact, Cormier believes that "the tougher they are, the better the project gets."[79] Indeed, he has worked relentlessly to push through his ideas for high-profile public spaces. Educational lectures appear to be fundamental to his tactics of persuasion. When members of the Waterfront Design Review Panel made scurrilous remarks about the pink umbrellas for Sugar Beach in Toronto, Cormier fought back and swayed the panel with a lecture on pink, including the use of pink by Jacqueline Kennedy when she was America's First Lady [183]. He showed slides of how she often dressed in pink and "looked elegant and respectful, but she also stood out and was expressing herself."[80] The review panel relented and the pink umbrellas today express their sugary context.

The dogs at Berczy Park were rejected at first because it was believed that dogs and art have nothing to do with one another. This critique prompted Cormier to educate the design review panel with a hundred slides documenting the extensive and persistent history of dogs in art. Dogs, in fact, have been a feature in much art throughout history.[81] But Cormier also battled for the paving pattern at Berczy Park, which one critic deemed too bold for Toronto, too strong [184]. The geometric paving pattern, composed of white, gray, and red pavers, proposed by Cormier was designed to pay homage to the neighborhood's historical red brick and gray stone buildings. Cormier pointed out that the paving pattern was based on the paving at the plaza fronting the Church of San Giorgio Maggiore in Venice [185]. He told the critic to also look at the lobby of Toronto's first City Hall, a much beloved heritage building. The lobby flooring of this building is stunning and bold. If strong paving patterns were not too bold for sixteenth-century Venetians or nineteenth-century Torontonians, why were they now too bold? The critic

78 Cormier and Parent, interview with Treib and Herrington, 9 July 2017.

79 Cormier, interview with Herrington, 6 April 2018.

80 Cormier and Parent, interview with Treib and Herrington, 9 July 2017.

81 Cormier, interview with Herrington, 18 August 2018.

THE CANADIAN STAG

184
Berczy Park.
Toronto, Ontario, 2017.
The bold paving pattern
is evident in this
aerial view.
[Industryous Photography]

185
Plaza outside
the Church of San Giorgio
Maggiore.
Venice, Italy, 2018.
[Yannick Roberge]

never mentioned paving again.[82] As installed, the paving pattern is reminiscent of the historic buildings in the surrounding neighborhood, and its complex geometry works well against the uniform expanses of grass and trees in the park.

Cormier consistently uses humor to sway review panels. When a member of the Waterfront Design Review Panel complained that the umbrellas planned for Sugar Beach were too small for his family and that "they would never come down to use the beach," Cormier mailed him a Christmas card.[83] The card displayed a model of the umbrella prototype planned for Sugar Beach. Under its canopy sat figurines of the Holy Family replete with the three wise men [**186**]. The member conceded and now enjoys taking his family to Sugar Beach.

Cormier also stresses the importance of working with clients and patrons as advocates for the project. "When the client works against you, that's not healthy. A good client supports you and does not punish you. It becomes a joy to work and you work harder: it's a win-win situation. I have learned that if the client wants you to lose, just get out. Both sides need to be supportive. A good client is also a champion for the project. No champion, no project."[84] This was certainly true of long-time Toronto city councilwoman Pam McConnell, who died in 2017, eight days after the opening of Sugar Beach [**187**]. Cormier described her as "a city builder who was working to make the world better."[85] Her support of both Sugar Beach and Berczy Park in Toronto was instrumental in their realization.

Sometimes champions emerge from surprisingly unlikely places. One afternoon a man was resting in the garden designed by Claude Cormier et Associés at the Four Seasons Hotel and Residences in downtown Toronto. For no apparent reason, he was kicked out of the garden by the hotel's security guards. As luck would have it, the man was a prominent member of Toronto's City Planning Division at the time, and he was offended by this treatment. The garden was intended, permitted, and approved as a privately owned public space. The incident gave city planners and Claude Cormier et Associés the opportunity to install the

82 Cormier, interview with Herrington, 25 July 2018.

83 Cormier, interview with Herrington, 18 August 2018.

84 Cormier, interview with Herrington, 6 April 2018.

85 Ibid.

186
Sugar Beach
Christmas card.
Toronto, Ontario, 2010.
The Holy Family
with the three wise men
taking refuge under
a Sugar Beach umbrella.
[Claude Cormier
et Associés]

187
Berczy Park.
Toronto, Ontario, 2017.
Opening day of the park
with Claude Cormier
and Pam McConnell
(red scarf).
[Industryous Photography]

red reclining chairs that had been originally envisioned by Cormier for the garden. Moreover, the addition of these chairs increased the garden's use by the public.[86]

This tension between private and public accessibility is a problem faced by many architects and landscape architects. Beautiful images of a proposed landscape are shown to the public by a developer hoping for additional increased floor area or other zoning modifications in exchange for this amenity. Although the landscape architect works hard to create a pleasant space for people, after the project is constructed and occupied, the owners often subject the landscape to a tyranny of surveillance maneuvers that greatly deter its use by the public. The Four Seasons project is an excellent example of the successful collaboration of a landscape architect working with city planners to ensure access to privately managed public spaces.

Listening to Communities

Among his manifold roles, Cormier likes to consider himself something of a social lubricant when working with the public. As Elsa Lam, editor at *Canadian Architect*, notes, "Beyond his design ability, Cormier is perhaps exceptional in his talent for building consensus around strong conceptual ideas."[87] Lam describes Claude Cormier et Associés' public process for the proposed Four Seasons Hotel and Residences landscape. At the start, the architects were planning two towers, thirty-eight and fifty-seven stories in height, situated in an old Victorian neighborhood in Toronto. Cormier knew people feared the scale and density of these towers, and how the glass and steel architecture clashed with their traditional two-story brick houses.

To quell these fears, he proposed a landscape to mediate this Victorian-meets-twenty-first-century confuddle. A three-story cast-iron fountain would address the towering scale of the hotel—its design inspired by Victorian-era fountains and meant to resonate with the character of the older residential structures [**188**]. The fountain sits in the center of the hotel's drop-off area, which is surfaced with colored pavers that create a giant vintage doormat replete with floral sprigs of roses at its edges. To soften the hardness of the glass and steel architecture, Cormier continued the floral theme with an adjacent garden graced by planting beds whose plan resembled the pattern of the folded petals of a rose. Both the hotel and the locals liked the scheme [**189**]. According to Steve Daniel, a former Toronto city planner, "When Claude presented his landscape design for the project, it deflected some of the controversy. ...It had a wow effect, and people bought into it."[88]

This approach is surely how Claude Cormier et Associés has been able to mine the inner workings of a community to feed the conceptual direction of a project. "We are always transparent," states Cormier, "and when I work with community groups, I pick up what is important to them. People are smart. You have to listen and to observe. By listening carefully, you can translate those desires into something bigger. Don't ask people to design a park—that is your task—but talk to them, ask them what they wish for, explain your ideas to them. You need to establish trust and then guide the process slowly to lead them to your vision. Don't hit them over the head with your ideas."[89] Cormier's approach to designing

86 Email correspondence with Georges-Étienne Parent in conversation with Marc Hallé, 23 July 2018.

87 Elsa Lam, "Collaborating with Cormier's Team: Recent Designs for Toronto," *ARQ: Architecture-Québec*, no. 139, May 2007, p. 22.

88 Quoted in Lam, "Collaborating with Cormier's Team," p. 21.

89 Cormier and Parent, interview with Treib and Herrington, 9 July 2017.

188
Four Seasons Hotel
and Residences.
Toronto, Ontario, 2012.
Section in neighborhood
context.
[Claude Cormier
et Associés]

189
Four Seasons Hotel
and Residences.
Plan.
[Claude Cormier
et Associés]

190
Latona Fountain.
Versailles, France, 2017.
[Zairon, Wikimedia Commons]

with communities comes from an unlikely source—a friend and former Deloitte accountant who worked on very complex financial transactions, and who served as an early role model for Cormier. The friend advised him to "pay attention to people; listen."[90]

Berczy Park in Toronto is an excellent example of this approach. During their initial meetings with the local community members, Cormier and his team noticed the constant presence of dog walkers. Although an off-leash area was required as part of the reprogramming of the park, the team had no idea that dogs and dog walkers were among the park's most avid users. When re-envisioning the park's former fountain, Cormier based his new design on the Latona Fountain in the gardens of Versailles. The three-tiered fountain is crowned by a statute of the Roman goddess of motherhood with her children [190]. Surrounding them, over fifty gilded frogs and other amphibians spurt water from their open mouths. The Versailles fountain captures the mythic moment when Latona cursed the peasants who stomped their feet, stirring up silt so her children couldn't drink the dirty water, and turned them into amphibians. Remembering the dog walkers and their interest in the park's revival plans, as well as the children and parents who also use Berczy Park, Cormier substituted dogs for frogs. On the top tier of the Berczy Fountain, he replaced the goddess Latona and her children with a golden bone, the Holy Grail of all canines.

The Cormier team worked intently with the community to identify the twenty-seven different dog breeds used for the fountain [191]. According to David Dick-Agnew, "The choice of which breeds to include drew passionate involvement from local residents, as you'd expect: We heard, do you have a terrier? Do you have a dachshund?"[91] During this process one woman complained with temerity, "Hey, why no cats?" So Cormier added two cats, one atop the electrical box where it watches the Sony Centre for Performing Arts across the street. The other sits on the fountain ledge unfazed by the antics of the dogs, its eyes turned to the two birds atop the nearby lamppost [192]. The treatment of the dogs took a longer time to determine. Initially envisioned as being one color, this all changed one day when Cormier visited his father's grave in Plessisville, Québec. Standing in the family graveyard, he looked up to see a life-size statue of the Virgin Mary. She was realistically painted in a high-gloss finish. Obviously, the dogs must

90 Ibid.

91 David Dick-Agnew, "5 Re-Imagined Landscapes by Claude Cormier," *Azure Magazine*, 27 June 2014, https://www.azuremagazine.com/article/works-claude-cormier/.

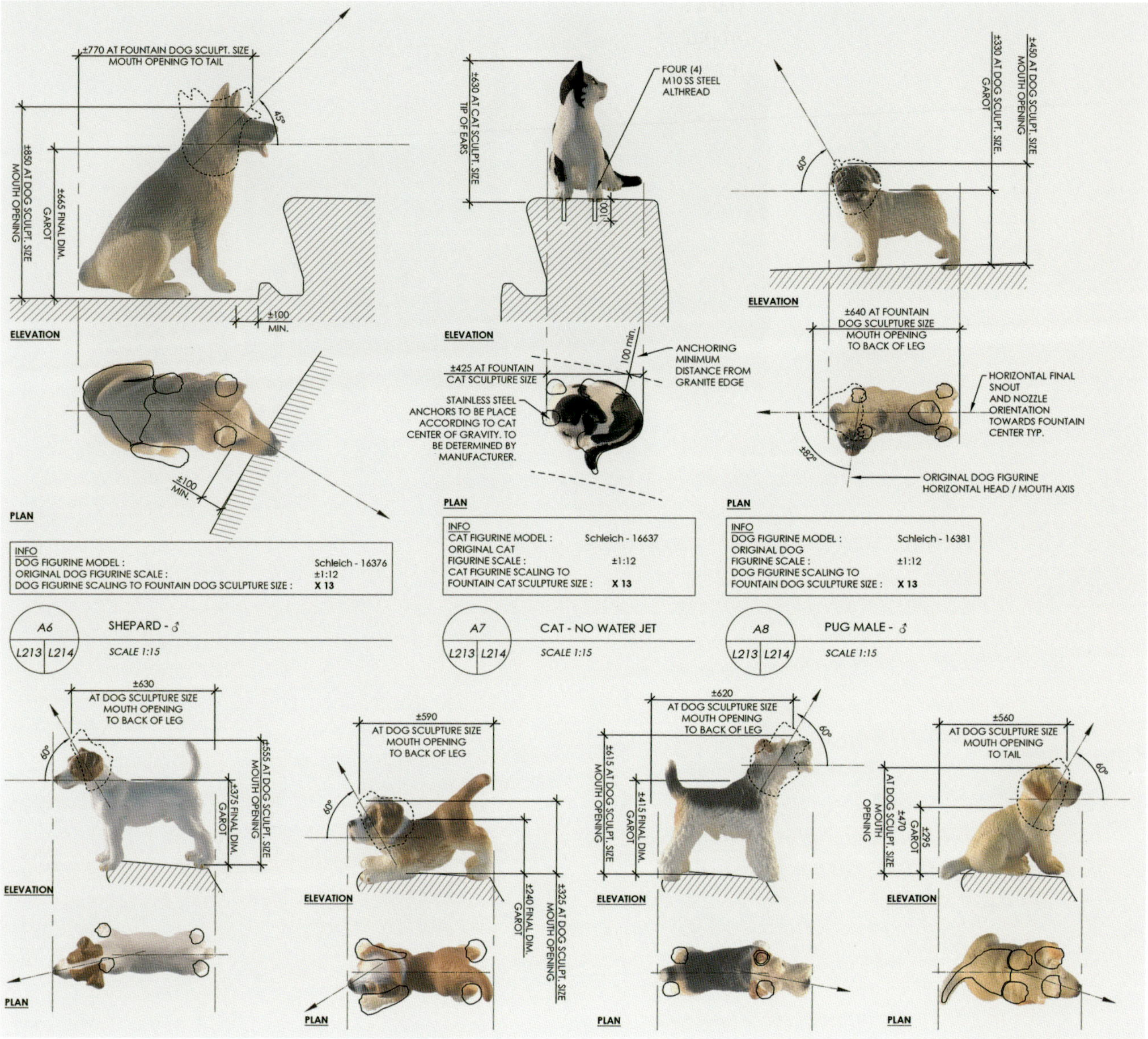

±770 AT FOUNTAIN DOG SCULPT. SIZE
MOUTH OPENING TO TAIL

45°

±850 AT DOG SCULPT. SIZE
MOUTH OPENING

±665 FINAL DIM.
GAROT

±100
MIN.

ELEVATION

±100
MIN.

PLAN

INFO
DOG FIGURINE MODEL : Schleich - 16376
ORIGINAL DOG FIGURINE SCALE : ±1:12
DOG FIGURINE SCALING TO FOUNTAIN DOG SCULPTURE SIZE : X 13

A6 L213 L214 SHEPARD - ♂
SCALE 1:15

±630 AT CAT SCULPT. SIZE
TIP OF EARS

FOUR (4)
M10 SS STEEL
ALTHREAD

100

ELEVATION

±425 AT FOUNTAIN
CAT SCULPTURE SIZE

100 min.

ANCHORING
MINIMUM
DISTANCE FROM
GRANITE EDGE

STAINLESS STEEL
ANCHORS TO BE PLACE
ACCORDING TO CAT
CENTER OF GRAVITY. TO
BE DETERMINED BY
MANUFACTURER.

PLAN

INFO
CAT FIGURINE MODEL : Schleich - 16637
ORIGINAL CAT
FIGURINE SCALE : ±1:12
CAT FIGURINE SCALING TO
FOUNTAIN CAT SCULPTURE SIZE : X 13

A7 L213 L214 CAT - NO WATER JET
SCALE 1:15

60°

±450 AT DOG SCULPT. SIZE
MOUTH OPENING

±330 AT DOG SCULPT. SIZE
GAROT

ELEVATION

±640 AT FOUNTAIN
DOG SCULPTURE SIZE
MOUTH OPENING
TO BACK OF LEG

HORIZONTAL FINAL
SNOUT
AND NOZZLE
ORIENTATION
TOWARDS FOUNTAIN
CENTER TYP.

±82°

ORIGINAL DOG FIGURINE
HORIZONTAL HEAD / MOUTH AXIS

PLAN

INFO
DOG FIGURINE MODEL : Schleich - 16381
ORIGINAL DOG
FIGURINE SCALE : ±1:12
DOG FIGURINE SCALING TO
FOUNTAIN DOG SCULPTURE SIZE : X 13

A8 L213 L214 PUG MALE - ♂
SCALE 1:15

±630
AT DOG SCULPTURE SIZE
MOUTH OPENING
TO BACK OF LEG

60°

±555 AT DOG SCULPT. SIZE
MOUTH OPENING

±375 FINAL DIM.
GAROT

ELEVATION

PLAN

±590
AT DOG SCULPTURE SIZE
MOUTH OPENING
TO BACK OF LEG

60°

±240 FINAL DIM.
GAROT

±325 AT DOG SCULPT. SIZE
MOUTH OPENING

ELEVATION

PLAN

±620
AT DOG SCULPTURE SIZE
MOUTH OPENING
TO BACK OF LEG

60°

±615 AT DOG SCULPT. SIZE
MOUTH OPENING

±415 FINAL DIM.
GAROT

ELEVATION

PLAN

±560
AT DOG SCULPTURE SIZE
MOUTH OPENING
TO TAIL

60°

±470
AT DOG SCULPT. SIZE
MOUTH
OPENING

±295
GAROT

ELEVATION

PLAN

191
(opposite, above)
Berczy Park.
Toronto, Ontario, 2013.
Working drawings
for the dogs.
[Claude Cormier
et Associés]

192
(opposite, below)
Berczy Park.
Toronto, Ontario, 2017.
The Birds.
[Industryous Photography]

193
Berczy Park.
Dog play.
[Industryous Photography]

194
(overleaf above)
The Well.
Toronto, Ontario, 2017.
The Well master plan.
[Claude Cormier
et Associés]

195
(overleaf below)
The Well.
West End cats,
East End dogs.
[Claude Cormier
et Associés]

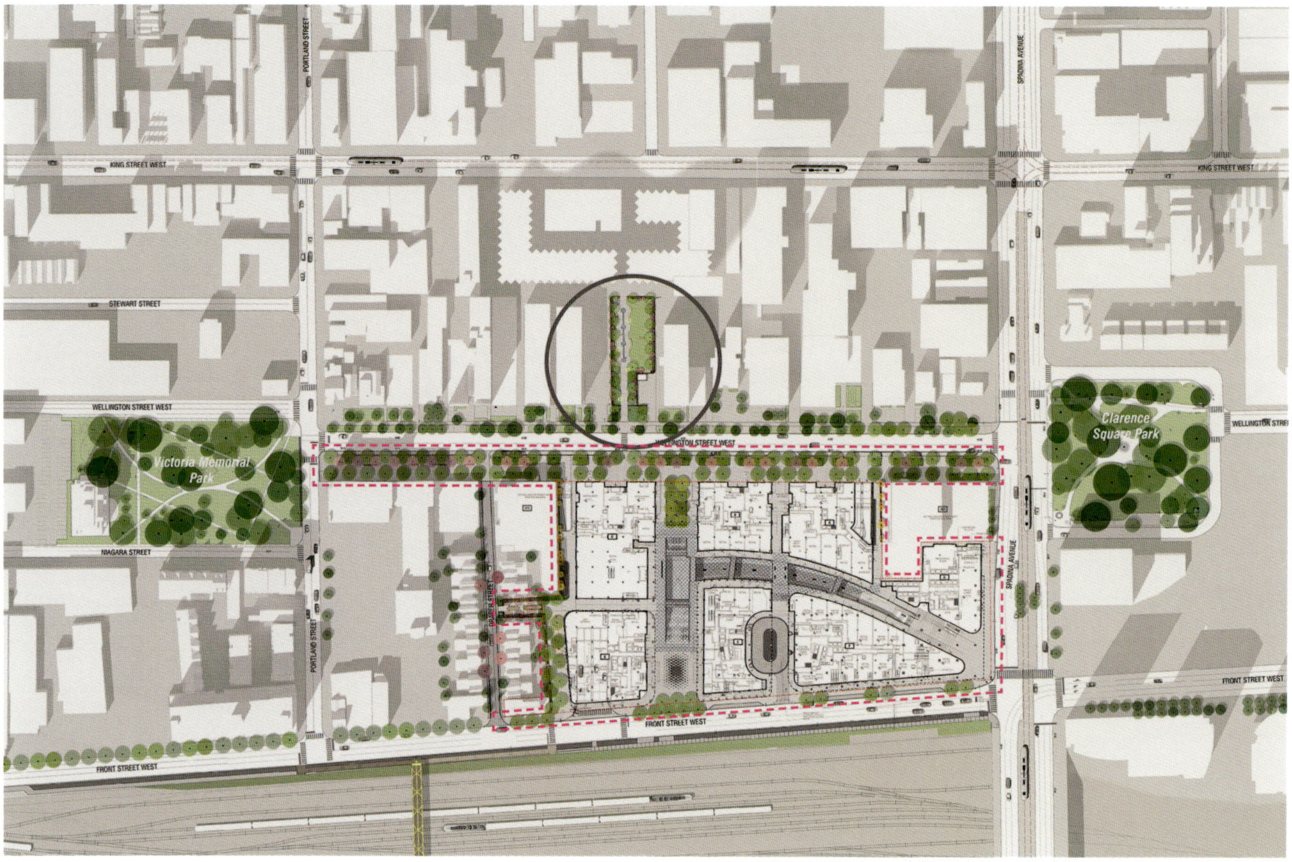

KING STREET WEST
PORTLAND STREET
SPADINA AVENUE
KING STREET WEST
STEWART STREET
WELLINGTON STREET WEST
Victoria Memorial Park
WELLINGTON STREET WEST
Clarence Square Park
NIAGARA STREET
FRONT STREET WEST
FRONT STREET WEST
FRONT STREET WEST

West End Cats
East End Dogs
Yonge Street
BERCZY PARK
WELLINGTON PLACE NEIGHBORHOOD
ST. LAWRENCE NEIGHBORHOOD

196
Dizzy the Cat.
Toronto, Ontario, 2017.
[Guillaume Paradis,
Claude Cormier et Associés]

be painted in the same way, and today the dogs sport an ecclesiastical sheen.[92]

The fountain is immensely popular with dog walkers and children, adults on their lunch break, as well as tourists [193]. In fact, the only people who seem disrespectful of Berczy Park are skateboarders. Around the seating edge of the last tier of the fountain, Cormier specified hundreds of studs to make it resemble a dog collar, but he also did this to stave off skateboarders in the area who have more than once tried to take over the park. As of this writing they have already broken one paw. Nonetheless, oodles of dogs lap up water in the very serviceable drinking trough at the base of the fountain, smaller children ride the dog sculptures or try to stop the water streaming from the dogs' mouths—and there is picture-taking aplenty. While it is uncertain how long the dogs will last with all this frenzied interaction, Cormier and his witty crew have continued the pet meme and their careful understanding of context and community at the Wellington Cat Promenade, also in Toronto.

While this project is still in the construction phase, the process behind the Wellington Cat Promenade reveals Cormier's deep reading of a place. Located west of Berczy Park, the promenade is part of the redevelopment of the former Globe and Mail building, which was demolished in 2017. The new 6.5-acre mixed-use development, the Well, includes a tree-lined promenade with plantings and public terraces that restore the link between Clarence Square Park to the east and Victoria Memorial Park to the west—a connection lost long ago with the construction of the Globe and Mail building and its vast parking lot [194]. Extending from this new promenade and connecting it to Wellington Street West, Cormier's 560-feet-long park, inspired by Dizzy the Cat, is in the works [195]. Another park, Draper Street Park, has also been planned to connect the Well site with Draper Street and is also dedicated to Dizzy.

Dizzy, an elderly white and yellow feline, is a very unusual denizen of the site [196]. I've met Dizzy and I have numerous images of Dizzy on my phone because my son worked near the Well site and during the summer, he and the cat ate lunch together almost every day. Certainly my son was not Dizzy's only dining partner as the pleasantly plump feline was well known in the neighborhood. According to Cormier, "We happened to always see the same cat on Draper Street hanging out in that little parkette. …He's a very nice, friendly cat, and for years he's always hanging out on that bench."[93] Cormier decided that Dizzy would be his muse for

92 Cormier, interview with Herrington, 21 June 2018.

93 Taylor Simmons, "Cat-themed parks to replace nightclub in Wellington Street West Neighbourhood," *CBC News*, 20 June 2018, https://www.cbc.ca/news/canada/toronto/cat-themed-parks-wellington-street-west-1.4713356.

the two small parks built as part of the Well development.

Plans are afoot to create two sets of paired larger-than-life statues of Dizzy, rendered in full color and high gloss, on either end of Wellington Street West Park. A linear pool, accompanied by plants such as catnip, black locusts, and trees with birdhouses are also envisioned. As a wink and a nudge to Berczy Park, there will also be one dog to accompany the dozens of life-size creatures that will include cats, birds, and a mouse or two [197]. The Draper Street Park will have similar figures but will also contain a long communal picnic table in place of a pool. While these parks are still under construction, news about the projects and Dizzy himself have captured the imagination of the press and Twitter users alike. In an interview with the Canadian Broadcasting Corporation, Cormier described these new parks as "whimsical. ...People love it and people seem to embrace it and they seem to want more of those moments in our cities."[94] Indeed, many of the landscapes produced by Claude Cormier et Associés offer a sociable moment in the urban environment.

Working the Crowd

In the eleventh chapter of his classic text, *The Social Life of Small Urban Spaces*, William H. Whyte introduces readers to his Theory of Triangulation: "By this I mean that process by which some external stimulus provides a linkage between people and prompts strangers to talk to each other as though they were not."[95] This external stimulus, Whyte notes, can be a physical object or sight, such as particular views, street characters in costumes, Jean Dubuffet's stainless steel *Rag Lady*, adroit acrobats, or a mime working in tandem with an itinerant cop.[96] But is a landscape's design capable of providing such stimuli?

Had Whyte lived to witness the works of Claude Cormier et Associés, surely he would have found them packed with triangulation. One exquisite example of Whyte's theory is Pink Balls, an installation suspended above thirteen blocks of rue Sainte-Catherine Est in Montréal during the summer months of 2011 to 2016 [198]. Pink Balls had a significant impact of the social life of this part of Montréal, called Gay Village. In summer, locals and visitors alike routinely gravitated to rue Sainte-Catherine Est to experience the installation: strangers smiled at the pink sky, commented to each other, and took photographs. Others delighted at the filigree of pink that floated swimmingly over their heads. Much of this pleasure stemmed from the collective pinkness resonating from the layers of 170,000-plus pink balls, whose buoyancy overhead increased the project's color reflectivity. Much in keeping with Bernard Lassus's *espace propre* theory, the balls color the air [199].[97]

Positive exchanges among people improve the sociability of the street, or what Whyte called the "river of life." Pink Balls also has had an artistic ripple effect within the Gay Village as it inspired artists to create other works in the area. For example, an artist installed a blue stairway to provide people with a view above the linear corridor of pink; another artist crafted pink and black polka-dotted trash bags for all the shop owners to use, and the project has even inspired several short videos in homage to Pink Balls.

In 2017 Claude Cormier et Associés redesigned Pink Balls as 18 Shades of Gay. With more balls than ever before, Cormier's

94 Ibid.

95 William H. Whyte, *The Social Life of Small Urban Spaces*, Washington, DC: Conservation Foundation, 1980, p. 94.

96 Ibid.

97 Susan Herrington, *Landscape Theory in Design*, London: Routledge, 2017, p. 74.

197
The Well.
Toronto, Ontario, 2017.
Visualization of
courtyard.
[Claude Cormier
et Associés]

EGLISE

198
(opposite)
Pink Balls.
Montréal, Québec, 2011.
Pink Balls on Sainte-Catherine Street East.
[Marc Cramer]

199
Pink Balls.
Pink Balls color the air.
[Marc Cramer]

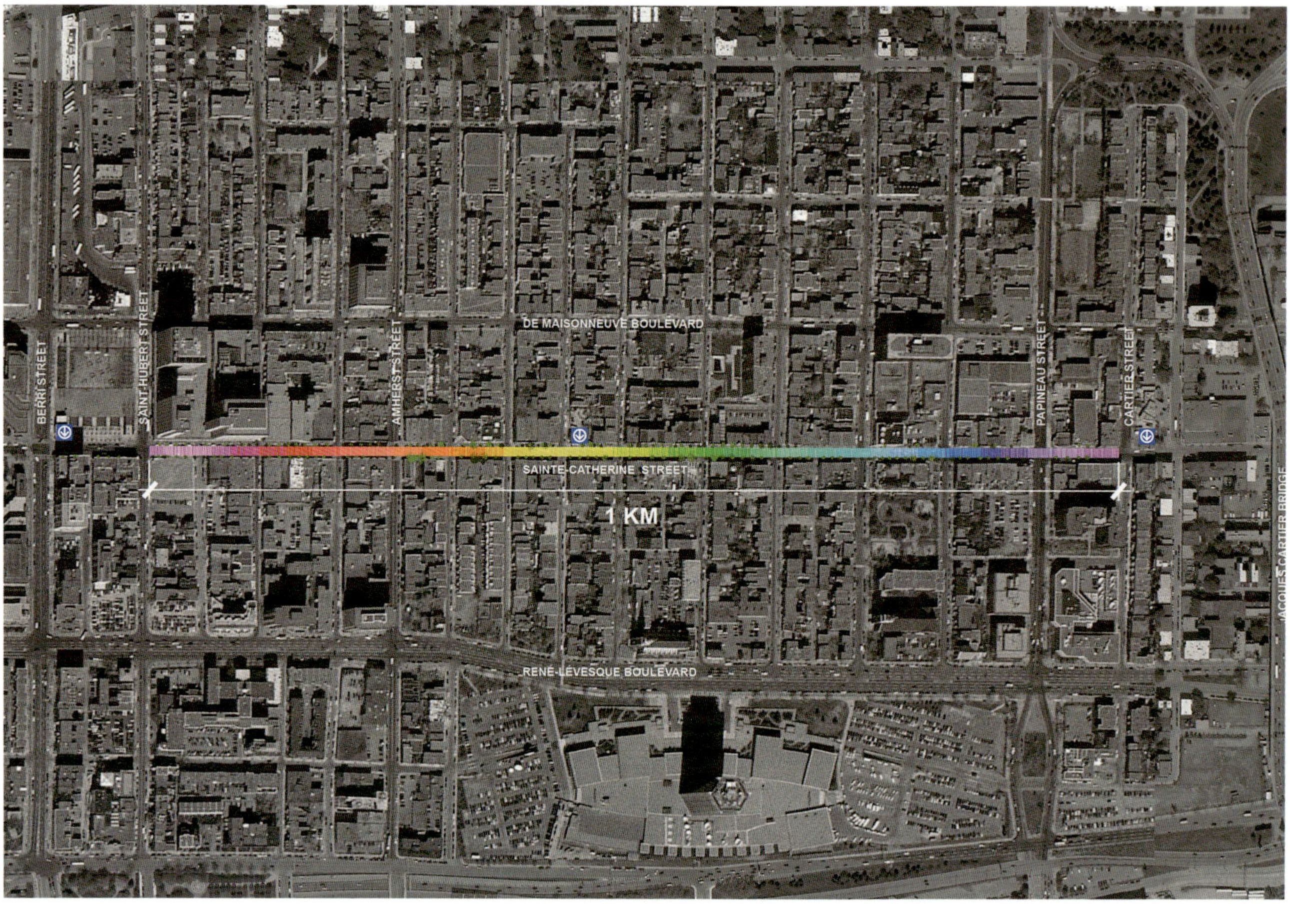

DE MAISONNEUVE BOULEVARD
BERRI STREET
SAINT-HUBERT STREET
AMHERST STREET
PAPINEAU STREET
CARTIER STREET
SAINTE-CATHERINE STREET
1 KM
RENÉ-LÉVESQUE BOULEVARD
JACQUES-CARTIER BRIDGE

200
(opposite)
18 Shades of Gay.
Montréal, Québec, 2017.
Developing the color scheme.
[Claude Cormier et Associés]

201
18 Shades of Gay.
Street views.
[Jean-Michael Seminaro]

202
"We've Got Balls" campaign.
Toronto, Ontario, 2018.
[Tourisme Montréal, Marine Intartaglia]

203
"We've Got Balls" campaign.
[Tourisme Montréal, Marine Intartaglia]

180,000 recycled plastic balls reference the first rainbow flag, originally designed by the San Francisco artist Gilbert Baker. Baker's flag comprised six stripes: red, orange, yellow, green, blue, and violet. In order to strengthen the optical effects of the balls and their ability to color the air, Cormier increased their tonal value in the same way that he increased the reflectivity of Pink Balls by using a high value shade of pink [**200**]. Cormier raised the tonal value of each color in the flag so that

Red becomes pink pastel
Blue becomes baby blue
Purple becomes lilac
Green becomes apple green
Orange becomes peach
Yellow becomes a lemon yellow

The opening of 18 Shades of Gay welcomed huge crowds in 2017 [**201**]. When Cormier declined to create a 2018 version of 18 Shades of Gay, a petition was promptly commenced to ensure that Cormier would reinstate the project. After all, Tourisme Montréal had launched its 2018 marketing campaign featuring the project. With the slogan "We've Got Balls. Come let your pride hang out," aerial images of 18 Shades of Gay were promoted in Toronto, New York, and throughout California [**202**] [**203**]. This time Cormier conceded, and 18 Shades of Gay graced the streets of Montréal once again in 2018.[98]

Claude Cormier et Associés also benefits from a form of triangulation unavailable to William H. Whyte: social media. Images of people pictured with the suspended balls, the pink tree trunks, the spurting dogs, and the pink umbrellas abound on the internet. Berczy Park has a Facebook page and Breakwater Park in Kingston, Ontario, has a live webcam. In 2016 Lipstick Forest was ranked one of the top ten Instagrammed sites in Montréal. The TOM series is a regular feature on TripAdvisor. Blue Stick Garden has been pinned and repinned many times on Pinterest with names as diverse as street art and blue flowers. On Vimeo you can watch a music video by Ubique Media about the Gay Village, inspired by and starring the Pink Balls.[99]

Claude Cormier's landscapes prompt triangulation because the stimuli he provides, while surprising and unusual in themselves, are informed by a deep reading of the place, and people's interpretation of his work is another form of its beauty. Cormier gleans these interpretations both through extensive research, sometimes of a historical nature, and by listening to members of the local community. This has made Cormier a desirable collaborator for projects that need a thoughtful focus and perhaps even some fun.

Collaborating with Design Teams

Much of Cormier's time and energy is spent introducing fun into the approval process, but he is also known for injecting levity into the design process with collaborators. In 2000, at the inauguration of the Métis International Garden Festival, the entire Cormier office donned blue cowboy hats in homage to the Blue Stick Garden and the Himalayan blue poppy [**204**]. Three years later Claude Cormier et Associés commenced a proposal with ENVision—The Hough Group and ERA Architects for the Toronto Waterfront Revitalization Corporation. The Commissioners Park project was to convert a forty-one-acre former industrial and munitions site in Toronto to public use. To mask the site's history of munitions manufacturing, Cormier conceived the idea of appropriating camouflage as the project's

98 Cormier, interview with Herrington, 18 August 2018.

99 Ubique Media, 2011, https://vimeo.com/27117847.

204
(opposite)
Blue Stick Garden.
Jardins de Métis/Reford
Gardens, Québec, 2000.
Blue cowboy hats for
the opening.
[Claude Cormier
et Associés]

205
Camouflage Park.
Toronto, Ontario, 2003.
Concept plan.
[Claude Cormier
et Associés]

206
Don Valley Brick Works. Toronto, Ontario, 1952. Looking south from Chorley Park. [James Victor Salmon, Public domain]

metaphor [205]. According to ERA Architects principal Michael McClelland, "One day, Claude and [coworker] Marc Hallé came into a meeting dressed in camouflage gear. ...I guess they wanted to make sure we got the idea—and picked up on the fun of it."[100] While they did not receive the commission, McClelland would involve Cormier in another major project, Evergreen Brick Works.

In 2006 McClelland and ERA were competing for the Evergreen Brick Works commission. For over a decade, the site sat "abandoned leaving behind a damaged ecosystem, crumbling buildings and contaminated soil."[101] The environmental nonprofit Evergreen purchased Don Valley Brick Works for one dollar with the aim of cleaning up the site and renovating the structures and landscape. Heritage was critical, too, as the factory had provided the bricks for important buildings in the city of Toronto for almost one hundred years [206]. Yet sustainability was another major concern. Evergreen's basic mandate for the project was to provide "a global showcase for green design, urban sustainability and a vibrant public space."[102]

McClelland explained that Evergreen wanted nature everywhere—everything needed to be green: "They were thinking of 'green' like the vegetables you're supposed to eat—not as something fun. I felt that what they really needed was Claude. He would be the conceptual lead on the team—to give priorities and explain the project."[103] When the team presented its proposal, Cormier commenced with a collaged image of the site that featured the loveable giant-sized vegetable company mascot, the Jolly Green Giant, towering over both the land and Toronto's emblematic CN Tower in the distance. Elsa Lam explains that in that slide, Cormier "presented a clear image of the Brick Works as an iconic presence in the landscape" and "that the team had a sense of humour, was quick-witted, and was able to commit to clear common values [207]."[104]

All this wit and camp is unique to a Canadian context. While landscape architects such as Ken Smith and Martha Schwartz have also engaged humor in both their design processes and end products, Cormier is distinctive among his Canadian peers. And this approach has paid off. The Evergreen Brick Works that Torontonians enjoy today is an extremely popular eco-art, environmental center that offers engaging programming and venues. One of the most

100 Quoted in Lam, "Collaborating with Cormier's Team," p. 20.

101 "Evergreen Brick Works: Visitors Guide," Evergreen, 2017, p. 1.

102 Ibid.

103 Quoted in Lam, "Collaborating with Cormier's Team," p. 22.

104 Ibid., p. 23.

207
Evergreen Brick Works.
Toronto, Ontario, 2006.
Conceptual visualizations.
[Claude Cormier
et Associés]

entertaining spaces at Brick Works is the skating rink at the open-air structure called the Koerner Gardens. As we know, Evergreen wanted everything green, even the skating rink. Cormier designed islands of plant material. Children whiz around the now-mature plants, chasing each other. The plants also lend a sense of mystery to what is typically a sterile environment of only ice.

In Closing

I began this essay with the subject of beauty and some new explanations of beauty put forth by philosophers. With an acute attention to color and composition, and their perceptual effects, much of Cormier's work is formally beautiful. Yet many of his projects also reflect the beauty espoused by Scarry and Nehamas. For Scarry, when we proclaim something beautiful, whether a person, art, or something from daily life, it causes us to pause as we attempt to understand others. The gaggle of adults and children at the Berczy Park fountain, the picnics in Lipstick Forest, people marveling at the color of the balls bobbing overhead at 18 Shades of Gay, and the plush appeal of *Stuffed Animals*—all prompt the "triangulation" that results in many of Cormier landscapes. All this picture-taking and all this wanting more makes Cormier's work a sociable beauty.

For Alexander Nehamas, beauty is subjective and changes with time, and embraces everything that we love, are drawn to, and are fascinated by. Beauty is evoked as Cormier's landscapes become a means of expression, as he conveys something to you about the site or the site's history. Moreover, many of Cormier's urban projects communicate to people who are not physically in the landscape, but above it—in towers. Scrivener Court with its large grapefruit water feature, the welcome mat at the Four Seasons Hotel and Residences entry, the magnified petals of the courtyards of the Biological Sciences building at the University of Montreal, and the outline of the old church at the Place d'Armes are viewed by hundreds of people living in buildings surrounding these urban landscapes. People looking down from the surrounding buildings must wonder, why the grapefruit, the entry mat, flower petals, or the silhouette of an old church?

Sometimes Cormier's narratives are subtle and respectful, as in Dorchester Square and Place d'Youville; sometimes they are bold, as in the TOM series and Sugar Beach. Surely one caveat is that beauty is subjective and will be interpreted in different ways by different people—but I doubt very much that Cormier would want people to use and interpret his work in any one specific way. He's a steadfast postmodernist in this regard. This said, there is one project now afoot in the office of Claude Cormier et Associés that has a very specific message: love.

In 2018, Waterfront Toronto held a six-week-long competition for a bold new park called York Street Park. Claude Cormier et Associés was one of five teams shortlisted to submit a design for the new park. Acting as team leaders, they brainstormed with gh3* on architecture, Arup on engineering, and Lesley Johnstone, the public art strategist. In a former life, the two-acre site was one leaf of a cloverleaf off-ramp from the Gardiner Expressway, which was demolished in 2016–2017. Situated west of HtO Beach and east of Sugar Beach, the park site is only a block from Toronto Harbour. Yet a massing of skyscrapers and busy streets also surround the site. In their proposal, team Cormier describe their Love Park scheme as the alter ego to the numbing homogeneity of the area's glass and steel construction.

Their scheme is reminiscent of other Cormier landscapes, a serious treatment of plant life and the introduction of fun and affection for objects. Love Park incorporates forty-two new and eighteen existing trees in an oasis of new soil [208] [209]. With a nod

208
Love Park.
Toronto, Ontario, 2018.
Aerial visualization
of park in spring.
[Claude Cormier
et Associés]

209
Love Park.
Aerial visualization
of park in winter.
[Claude Cormier
et Associés]

210
(opposite)
Love Park.
Toronto, Ontario, 2018.
Visualization.
[Claude Cormier
et Associés]

211
Love Park.
Visualization of park
in fall.
[Claude Cormier
et Associés]

212
Love Park.
Toronto, Ontario, 2018.
Visualization featuring central pool in the form of a heart.
[Claude Cormier et Associés]

213
Love Park.
Toronto, Ontario, 2018.
Visualization showing
suspended heart.
[Claude Cormier
et Associés]

to the Well project, Cormier envisions a menagerie of animals for the park. With a camouflage finish, even the recycling containers of Love Park pay homage to the new forest.

The shimmering paving proposed is inspired by Dorchester Square (without the crosses, however) [210]. A heart-shaped basin is aligned with true north. Suspended above the pool floats an illuminated pink heart that promises to inspire "joy, hope, optimism, and a relaxing of personal space across all seasons [211] [212]."[105] And with a nod to triangulation, Claude Cormier et Associés added that, used as "a tool for wayfinding or an object of contemplation, the suspended heart becomes a jewel that reinforces the unique qualities and conceptual foundation for Love Park [213]."[106]

Their design scheme also claims to go beyond William Whyte's call for triangulation, perhaps to achieve a love triangle. "Love Park will become another urban catalyst, similar to our other Toronto projects—Sugar Beach and Berczy Park—that playfully compel people to give in to their heart's wish to just let themselves feel good."[107] Toronto needs Love Park, the year 2018 was marred by violence, and like many cities, Toronto continues to suffer from COVID-19.[108] Can a landscape express and promote love? Waterfront Toronto seems to think so. Love Park won the competition in October of 2018, and that's a beautiful thing.

105 Claude Cormier, *Love Park Toronto,* Proposal booklet, 26 June 2018, https://yorkreesparkdesign.ca/wp-content/uploads/RFP-2018-18-YSP-LOVE-PARK-PROPOSAL-BOOKLET_LR.pdf, p. 11.

106 Ibid., p. 32.

107 Ibid., p. 2

108 "Danforth Rampage Continues a Deadly Year of Gun Violence for Toronto," *The Canadian Press, CP24,*23 July 2018, https://www.cp24.com/news/danforth-rampage-continues-a-deadly-year-of-gun-violence-for-toronto-1.4023931.

Bibliography

The Making of Serious Fun

Lectures

Cormier, Claude. Isabella Stewart Gardner Museum, Boston, 22 September 2015.

————————. "Serious Fun." University of Toronto, Ontario, 31 May 2018. https://www.youtube.com/watch? v=fXIhtPhJgiE.

Publications

Abbott, Edwin A. *Flatland: A Romance of Many Dimensions*. London: Seeley, 1884.

Bowron, Edgar Peters, Carolyn Rose Rebbert, Robert Rosenblum, and William Secord. *Best in Show: The Dog in Art from the Renaissance to Today*. New Haven, CT: Yale University Press, 2006.

Calvino, Italo. *Invisible Cities*. Translated by William Weaver. New York: Harcourt Brace Jovanovich, 1974.

Danto, Arthur C. "Banality and Celebration: The Art of Jeff Koons." In *Jeff Koons: Retrospektiv/Retrospective*, edited by Marit Woltmann. Oslo: Astrup Fearnley Museum of Modern Art, 2004.

Eckbo, Garrett. *Landscape for Living*. New York: Duell, Sloan and Pearce, 1950.

Greenberg, Clement. *Art and Culture: Critical Essays*. Boston: Beacon, 1961.

Kearney, Mark, and Randy Ray. *The Big Book of Canadian Trivia*. Toronto: Dundurn, 2009.

Landecker, Heidi, ed. *Martha Schwartz: Transfiguration of the Commonplace*. Washington, DC: Spacemaker, 1996.

Lynes, Russell. *The Tastemakers: The Shaping of American Popular Taste*. New York: Harper and Brothers, 1955; reprint, New York: Dover, 1980.

Menninghaus, Winfried. "On the 'Vital Significance' of Kitsch: Walter Benjamin's Politics of 'Bad Taste'" (2009). In *Walter Benjamin and the Architecture of Modernity*, edited by Andrew Benjamin and Charles Rice. Melbourne: re.press, 2016.

Meyer, Elizabeth K. "The Public Park as Avante-Garde (Landscape) Architecture: A Comparative Interpretation of Two Parisian Parks, Parc de la Villette (1983–1990) and Parc des Buttes-Chaumont (1864–1867)." *Landscape Journal* 10, no. 1, Spring 1991.

Pickeral, Tamsin. *The Dog: 5000 Years of the Dog in Art*. New York: Merrell, 2008.

Powers, Alan. *The Bauhaus Goes West: Modern Art and Design in Britain and America*. London: Thames & Hudson, 2019.

Richardson, Tim, ed. *The Vanguard Landscapes and Gardens of Martha Schwartz*. London: Thames & Hudson, 2004.

Schjeldahl, Peter. "'Like Life' Shows Seven Hundred Years of the Body." *New Yorker*, 2 April 2018. https://www.newyorker.com/magazine/2018/04/02/like-life-shows-seven-hundred-years-of-the-body.

Smith, Ken. *Ken Smith: Landscape Architect*. New York: Monacelli, 2009.

Smith, William S. "The Weak and the Dead: What the Rise of KAWS Says about the Art World's Ailments." *Art in America* 107, no. 8, September 2019.

Sontag, Susan. *Against Interpretation*. New York: Farrar, Straus and Giroux, 1961.

Treib, Marc. "A Constellation of Pieces." *Landscape Architecture* 92, no. 3, March 2002.

Tunnard, Christopher. *Gardens in the Modern Landscape*. London: Architectural Press, 1938.

Varnedoe, Kirk, and Adam Gopnik. *High and Low: Modern Art and Popular Culture*. New York: Museum of Modern Art, 1990.

Venturi, Robert. *Complexity and Contradiction in Architecture.* New York: Museum of Modern Art, 1966.

Williams, Ron. *Landscape Architecture in Canada*. Montreal: McGill-Queen's University Press, 2014.

Woolf, Virginia. *The Death of the Moth and Other Essays*. Quoted in Hana Leaper, "Opinion: 'Middlebrow' Art," *Tate Etc.,* Spring 2018.

Websites

"Don Valley Brick Works." Wikipedia. https://en.wikipedia.org/wiki/Don_Valley_Brick_Works.

"Dorchester Square." Wikipedia. https://en.wikipedia.org/wiki/Dorchester_Square.

Evergreen Brick Works. https://www.evergreen.ca/evergreen-brick-works/.

Zimbio. https://www.zimbio.com/Dolly+Parton/articles/PyO3d-Z_Eqi/26+Dolly+Parton+Quotes+Prove+Cooler+Smarter.

The Beauty of Serious Fun

Cormier, Claude. "*The Burning of the Canadian Parliament in Montréal,* 1849." McCord Museum, Montreal, 17 March 2011. https://www.youtube.com/watch? v=2iedvsLhA1I.

——————. "Color Is Not a Decoration." P. H. Elwood Lecture, Iowa State University, Ames, Iowa, 17 October 2014. https://vimeo.com/109731946.

Publications

Beswick, Aaron. "Canada Turned Away Jewish Refugees." *The Chronicle Herald,* 15 December 2013. http://thechronicleherald.ca/novascotia/1174272-canada-turned-away-jewish-refugees.

"Big Bang—Giving Free Rein to Creativity" [Big Bang—Carte blanche à la créativité]. Montreal Museum of Fine Arts, 7 November 2011. https://translate.google.com/translate? hl=en&sl=fr&u=https://voir.ca/bigbang/2011/11/08/big-bang-carte-blanche-a-la-creativite/&prev=search.

Blossfeldt, Karl. *Urformen der Kunst* [Art Forms in Nature: Enlarged Photographs of Plant Forms]. New York: Universe Books, 1967.

Chevreul, Michel-Eugène. "The Principles of Harmony and Contrast of Colours, and Their Applications to the Arts," 448–66. In *Nineteenth-Century Theories of Art*, edited by Joshua C. Taylor. Berkeley: University of California Press, 1987.

Claude Cormier Architectes Paysagistes Inc., Groupe Cardinal Hardy, and Teknika-HBA. *Réaménagement et mise en valeur du square Dorchester et de la place du Canada,* 2016.

Cormier, Claude. *Love Park Toronto.* Proposal booklet, 26 June 2018. https://yorkreesparkdesign.ca/wp-content/uploads/RFP-2018-18-YSP-LOVE-PARK-PROPOSAL-BOOKLET_LR.pdf.

"Danforth Rampage Continues a Deadly Year of Gun Violence for Toronto." *The Canadian Press, CP24,* 23 July 2018. https://www.cp24.com/news/danforth-rampage-continues-a-deadly-year-of-gun-violence-for-toronto-1.4023931.

Dick-Agnew, David. "5 Re-Imagined Landscapes by Claude Cormier." *Azure Magazine*, 27 June 2014. https://www.azuremagazine.com/article/works-claude-cormier/.

Duffy, Andrew. "How an Ottawa Student's Outrage Led to the National Holocaust Monument." *Ottawa Citizen*, 6 September 2017. https://ottawacitizen.com/news/local-news/how-an-ottawa-students-outrage-led-to-the-national-holocaust-monument.

Edwards, Jennifer. "Place d'Armes." *Infopresse*, 1 November 2007. https://www.infopresse.com/archive/article/24255.

Erwin, Norman. "The Holocaust, Canadian Jews, and Canada's 'Good War' Against Nazism." *Canadian Jewish Studies / Études juives canadiennes* 24, 2016.

Evergreen Brick Works: Visitors Guide. Evergreen, 2017.

Gilliam, James E. "The Effects of Baker-Miller Pink on Physiological and Cognitive Behavior of Emotionally Disturbed and Regular Education Students." *Behavioral Disorders* 17, no. 1, 1991.

Herrington, Susan. *Landscape Theory in Design*, London: Routledge, 2017.

Hougie, Chris. *Cornerstone: Festival of Gardens: New Frontiers in Modern Gardens.* Novato, CA: ORO Editions, 2005.

Howell, Steven. "Eclectic Installations." *Press-Republican*, 29 December 2011. http://www.pressrepublican.com/news/out_and__about/eclectic-installations/article_4fdc5ed5-f5d8-5f95-ac9b-bce808238ad4.html.

Jekyll, Gertrude. *Colour in the Flower Garden.* The "Country Life" Library. London, "Country Life"; George Newnes, 1908. http://www.gutenberg.org/files/50764/50764-h/50764-h.htm.

Lam, Elsa. "Collaborating with Cormier's Team: Recent Designs for Toronto," in *ARQ : Architecture-Québec*, no. 139, May 2007.

Ljubanovic, Kristina. "Favourite Room; Landscape Architect Claude Cormier's Montreal Home Is Just What You'd Expect—Playful and Engaging." *The Globe and Mail*, 25 January 2018. https://www.theglobeandmail.com/life/home-and-garden/decor/landscape-architects-Montréal-home/article37729370/.

Lopes, Dominic, and Matthew Kieran, eds. *Knowing Art: Essays in Aesthetics and Epistemology.* Philosophical Studies Series 107. Dordrecht: Springer Netherlands, 2006.

Lord, Gail Dexter, and Dov Goldstein. *Our Journey Toward Canada's Holocaust Monument: Personal Reflection by Gail Dexter Lord and Dov Goldstein.* Holocaust Monument Book. Lord Cultural Resources, [2017].

Marsan, Jean Claude. *Montreal in Evolution: Historical Analysis of Montreal's Architecture and Urban Environment.* Montreal: McGill-Queen's University Press, 1981.

Meyer, Elizabeth K. "Sustaining Beauty: The Performance of Appearance; A Manifesto in Three Parts." *Journal of Landscape Architecture* 3, no. 1, Spring 2008.

Morisset, Lucie K. "Of History and Memory: An Allegory of Identity in the Redevelopment of Place d'Youville (Montreal)." *Journal of the Society for the Study of Architecture in Canada* 25, nos. 2–4, 2000.

Nehamas, Alexander. *Only a Promise of Happiness: The Place of Beauty in a World of Art.* Princeton, NJ: Princeton University Press, 2007.

"Place d'Armes: Old Montreal's Public Square Cradle of City's Long History." *The Guardian*, 22 November 2011. http://www.theguardian.pe.ca/living/place-darmes-old-Montréals-public-square-cradle-of-citys-long-history-108901/.

Rao, Pragnya. "Nature Inspired Interiors: Out in the Open," What's Now: Design, Architecture & Art, *Elle Decor* (*India*), April–May 2009.

Richardson, Tim, ed. *The Vanguard Landscapes and Gardens of Martha Schwartz*. London: Thames & Hudson, 2004.

Riga, Andy. "Dorchester Square to Get a Victorian Fountain in Renovation Project." *Montréal Gazette*, 23 May 2018. https://Montréalgazette.com/news/local-news/dorchester-square-to-get-a-victorian-fountain-in-renovation-project.

Rose, Owen. "Claude Cormier." *The Fifth Column* 10, no. 4, 2002.

Sandler, Irving. *Abstract Expressionism and the American Experience: A Reevaluation.* Mission Critical Series. Lenox, MA: Hard Press Editions; New York: School of Visual Arts; Manchester, VT, in association with Hudson Hills Press, 2009.

Scarry, Elaine. *On Beauty and Being Just*. Princeton, NJ: Princeton University Press, 1999.

Schellekens, Elizabeth. "Conceptual Art." 22 October 2014. *The Stanford Encyclopedia of Philosophy.* http://plato.stanford.edu/archives/win2014/entries/conceptual-art.

Schneider, Sven Raphael. "Bottom Button Rules for Vest & Waistcoat." *Gentleman's Gazette*, 4 May 2010. https://www.gentlemansgazette.com/waiscoat-button/.

Simmons, Taylor. "Cat-themed Parks to Replace Nightclub in Wellington Street West Neighbourhood." *CBC News,* 20 June 2018. https://www.cbc.ca/news/canada/toronto/cat-themed-parks-wellington-street-west-1.4713356.

Solyom, Catherine. "Skeletal Remains Open Window to Our Past." *Montreal Gazette*, 9 October 2009. https://www.pressreader.com/canada/Montréal-gazette/20091009/281586646653149.

Theodore, David "Bright Lights, Big Price Tag: The New Palais des congrès Is Worth Every Cent." *Maisonneuve,* 1 March 2003. https://maisonneuve.org/article/2003/03/1/bright-lights-big-price-tag/.

Waugh, Emily. "Territories of Engagement" *Landscape Architecture's Core?* Special issue, *Harvard Design Magazine* 36, 2013.

Whyte, William H. *The Social Life of Small Urban Space*s. Washington, DC: Conservation Foundation, 1980.

Williams, Ron. *Landscape Architecture in Canada.* Montreal: McGill-Queen's University Press, 2014.

Wilson, R. D., and Eric McLean. *Montreal*. Montreal: McGill University Press, 1964.

Wolfe, Joshua, and Cécile Grenier. *Montreal Guide: An Architectural and Historical Guide*, Montreal: Libre Expression, 1983.

Websites

Cormier, Claude. "Place d'Youville, Montréal (Québec), Canada." Claude Cormier et Associés: Landscape Architecture and Urban Design. http://www.claudecormier.com/en/projet/place-dyouville/accessed.

Hustak, Alan. "Downtown Montréal—Phillips Square." Montréal Walking Tours, 2002. Véhicule Press. http://www.vehiculepress.com/Montréal/downtown.html.

"Place d'Armes." Répertoire du patrimoine culturel du Québec. Québec Culture et Communications 2005. http://www.patrimoine-culturel.gouv.qc.ca/rpcq/detail.do? methode=consulter&id=100097&type=bien#.Wz_Pyi0ZNgc.

Ubique Media, 2011, https://vimeo.com/27117847.

Project List

1990 *Enchanted Forest*, Montréal
—Nightclub landscape installation

© Bar Business

1992–2010 Canadian Centre for Architecture, Montréal
—Landscape management for the museum park and garden

1996–1998 J.-A.-DeSève Pavillon, Université du Québec à Montréal
—Landscape for new downtown academic complex

1997 *Blue Lawn*, Canadian Centre for Architecture, Montréal
—Lawn intervention

1997–1998 Square Phillips, Montréal
—Revitalization of a public square in the center city

1997–2008 Place d'Youville, Old Montréal
—National design competition winning entry for a new public space in the city's historic district

1997–2010 Benny Farm, Notre-Dame-de-Grâce, Montréal
—Landscape for a social housing development, executed in nine phases

1999 Sainte-Geneviève Escarpment, Québec City
—Improvements to the southern escarpment of Québec City

1999 *Red Lawn*, Los Angeles
—Installation at the Schindler House/ MAK Center, Los Angeles

1999–2000 Montreal Garden, Shanghai
—Abstract Canadian landscape,
Pudong Century Park

© Claude Cormier et Associés

1999–2002 *Lipstick Forest* and Esplanade,
Palais des congrès, Montréal
—Winter Garden and plaza

1999–2013 *Blue Stick Garden*
—Temporary installations
at these venues:

1999 Les Jardins de Métis,
Métis-sur-Mer, Québec

2004 Hestercombe Gardens,
Taunton, England

2006 Flora International,
Old Port of Montréal

2009 Métis-sur-Mer, Québec
(Permanent installation)

2013 Cool Gardens, Winnipeg,
Manitoba

2000–2003 Jacques Cartier Bridge Gateway,
Montréal
—Landscape and transportation
master plan

2001 Battersea Power Station, London,
England
—Redevelopment master plan
for the iconic Battersea site
for Cirque du Soleil

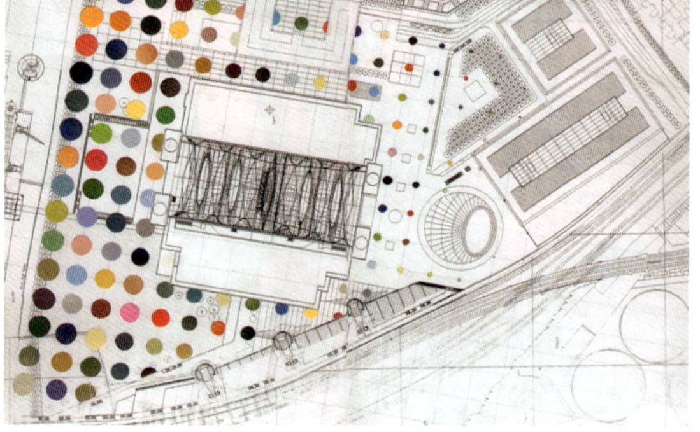

© Claude Cormier et Associés

2001–2003 Place des Arts, Montréal
—Plan for a performing arts center
and museum of contemporary art
for the public realm

© Claude Cormier et Associés

2002 Avenue du Parc/Avenue des Pins
Interchange, Montréal
—Urban design strategy for the
reconfiguration of the two-level urban
interchange

2002–2007 *Blue Forest*, Detroit, Michigan
—Courtyard designs for the Nissan
Design Studio

2003 International Mosaïcultures of
Montréal, Dubai, United Arab Emirates
—Master plan for a vegetal mosaiculture
festival

2003 *Solange*, Garden Biennale, Lyon, France
—Temporary installation of silk flowers in an ancient forest

© Claude Cormier et Associés

2003 Moonwalk, Las Vegas
—Landscape master plan for MGM Resorts/Cirque du Soleil hotel and casino

2003–2004 Camouflage Park/Commissioners Park, Toronto Waterfront
—Conceptual development for 41-acre brownfield site

2003–2005 Pierre-Dansereau Science Campus, Université du Québec à Montréal
—Landscape plan for the 2.8-acre life sciences campus in downtown Montréal

2003–2007 HtO Urban Beach, with Janet Rosenberg, Toronto Waterfront
—Urban beach and park on Toronto waterfront resulting from winning entry in an international design competition

2004–2005 *Blue Tree*, Cornerstone Festival of Gardens, Sonoma, California
—Landscape installation featuring a dead pine tree

2004–2005 Waterfront Park, Otterburn Park, Québec
—Study for a recreational river-edge landscape and a future beach

2004–2006 St. James Church, Montréal
—Plaza fronting the façade of a historic church on downtown Montréal's main street

2005–2006 Entrepôt Frigorifique, Old Port of Montréal
—River-edge promenade park

2005–2006 Jackie Gleason Theater, Miami Beach, Florida
—Master plan for the outdoor space accompanying the transformation of a historic theater for Cirque du Soleil

© Claude Cormier et Associés

2005–2007 University of Manitoba Institute for Advanced Medicine, Winnipeg
—Open space and interior artificial forest as winter garden

2005–2007 McGill University, Life Sciences Complex, Montreal
—Public landscape and green roof

2005–2009 University of Waterloo Pharmacy School, Kitchener, Ontario
—Landscape master plan and site design

2005–2010 Urban Prairie, Canadian Museum of History, Gatineau, Québec
—Public green plaza

© Michel Boulianne

2006 Contemporary Art Biennial, Le Havre, France
—Pergola art installation

2006–2008 Collège Ahuntsic, Montréal
—Landscape for student residences

2006–2009 Old Port of Montréal
—17-acre horticultural master plan

2006–2010 Evergreen Brick Works, Toronto
—Transformation of a 14-acre industrial brownfield to an environmental community center

2006–2012 Four Seasons Hotel and Residences, Toronto
—Public landscape for flagship hotel and residences

2006–2015 300 Front Street, Toronto
—Public park and streetscape design for two residential towers

2006–2016 Sony Centre for the Performing Arts and L Tower, Toronto
—Streetscape and urban plaza

© Industryous Photography

2007–2009 Viger DMC, Old Montréal
—Landscape design for mixed-use development

2007–2010 Sugar Beach, Toronto Waterfront
—Iconic urban beach and park

2007–2018 Backstage, Toronto
—Esplanade, roof terrace, and pool for residential tower

© Industryous Photography

2008 Pearl Morissette Estate Winery, Jordan, Niagara Valley, Ontario
—Landscape design for a new 42-acre vineyard

2008–2009 Old Port of Montréal
—Mobility and urban forestry master plan

2008–2012 Parc Hydro-Québec, Downtown Montréal
—Sustainable public park

2008–2019 Dorchester Square and Place du Canada, Montréal
—Phased master plan for revitalization of historic public spaces

2009 Relocation of the *Blue Forest* to Nissan Design Studio, La Jolla, California

2010 Gardiner Expressway and Lake Shore Boulevard reconfiguration, Toronto
—International design competition entry in collaboration with OMA / Arup

2010–2011 Leslie Nymark, Toronto
—Master plan for a 6.5-acre residential development with Toronto Community Housing Corporation

2010–2012 Clock Tower Beach, Old Port of Montréal
—Urban beach and environmentally planned parking area

2010–2016 117 Peter Street, Toronto
—Public spaces and rooftop for a residential tower development

2011–2013 3C Waterfront and Silo site, Toronto
—Master plan for a 13-acre mixed-use waterfront development

2011–2015 Performing Arts Centre and Brock University School of Fine and Performing Arts, St. Catharines, Ontario
—Public spaces for new downtown arts campus

2011–2019 Aires Libres: *Pink Balls / 18 Shades of Gay*, Montréal
—Kilometer-long annual pedestrian street installation for summer events (nine versions)

2012 *Les Peluches*, Montreal Museum of Fine Arts
—Artwork commissioned for the *Big Bang* exhibition. Now part of the museum's permanent collection

2012 Old Port of Montréal
—Landscape master plan for the 35-acre site

2012–2013 Le Château Apartments, Montréal
—Public spaces for residential complex

2012–2013 Evergreen Brick Works, Toronto
—Urban courtyards for a post-industrial brownfield site

2012–2014 *TOM I*, *TOM II*, and *TOM III*, Montreal Museum of Fine Arts
—Outdoor art installations using Traffic Overlay Markers (TOMs)

2012–2017 Distillery District Ribbon Building, Toronto
—Landscape master plan for mixed-use development in historic district

2012–2017 Ville Saint-Laurent Sports Complex, Montréal
—Landscape and public realm design

2012–2018 Breakwater Park, City of Kingston, Ontario
—Kilometer-long shoreline promenade along Lake Ontario and urban beach

2012–2018 Vaughan Metropolitan Centre, Vaughan, Ontario
—Landscape master plan with 10-acre urban park as its core

© Claude Cormier et Associés, Diamond Shmitt Architects

2012–2020 City of the Arts, Lower Jarvis Street, Toronto Waterfront
—From master plan to site construction for streetscape and public realm for 1.3-acre mixed-use development

2012–2020 The Selby, Toronto
—Public space and streetscape for a luxury residential tower

2012–2022 Garrison Point, Toronto
—Master plan for five-tower mixed-use residential district and 3-acre urban park on a former brownfield site

© Industryous Photography

2013–2014 *Trash*, Montréal
—Art installation on Sainte-Catherine Street accompanying *Pink Balls*

2013–2014 Royal Ontario Museum, Toronto
—Public realm design and streetscape improvement

2013–2015 *Au grand dam*, Ville LaSalle, Québec
—Winning entry in competition for public art for the Parc des Rapides.

© Yves Lacombe

2013–2017 National Holocaust Monument, Ottawa
—Landscape design in collaboration with Studio Daniel Libeskind, Edward Burtynsky, and Doris Bergen

2013–2017 Berczy Park, Toronto
—Winning entry, international design competition for the revitalization of an iconic fountain for historic downtown park

2013–2017 Parc Jean-Drapeau, Montréal
—Master plan and revitalization of the 63-acre Expo 67 site, celebrating 375th anniversary of the founding of Montréal and 50th anniversary of Expo 67

© Claude Cormier et Associés

2013–2017 Cité archéologique, Place d'Youville, Pointe-à-Callière Museum, Old Montréal
—Public landscape master plan design for the museum's extension

2013–2018 River City Phase 3, Toronto
—Public realm, private landscape, and roof amenities

2013–2023 The Well, Toronto
—Urban landscape master plan and implementation for a seven-tower mixed-use development of 9.5 acres

2014– L'Île-aux-Grues, Quebec
—Landscape plan for a 45-acre estate in Québec for a major art collector

2014–2015 LeBreton Flats Redevelopment, Ottawa
—Landscape master plan for 5.6-acre mixed-use development

2014–2015 Cirque du Soleil, Montréal
—Sculpture garden for Guy Laliberté's private collection at the Cirque du Soleil headquarters

2014–2017 King Portland Centre, Toronto
—Landscape and public realm for three-tower mixed-use development in a historic district

2014–2017 Frédéric Back Garden, Montreal Museum of Fine Arts
—Multifunctional rooftop public space and sculpture garden

2015–2022 88 Queen Street East, Toronto
—Public landscape and roof gardens for a 2.8-acre, four-tower mixed-use development

2015–2023 Canadian National Institute for the Blind, Edmonton, Alberta
—Public and rooftop landscapes within a residential tower development

2016–2017 *Balade pour la Paix*, Montreal Museum of Fine Arts
—Kilometer-long installation celebrating Montréal's 375th anniversary

2016–2021 Scrivener Square, Rosedale, Toronto
—Public street and courtyard landscapes for mixed-use residential development

© COBE Architects

2016–2021 Curtis Block, Downtown Calgary
—Landscape for three-tower mixed-use residential development

2016–2027 Commerce Court, Toronto
—Master plan and implementation for office towers in the heart of Toronto's financial district

© Hariri Pontarini Architects

2017– Lakeshore East, Chicago
—Private and public landscapes for 4-acre, three-tower residential development

© Claude Cormier et Associés, Lendlease, Magellan Development Group, bKL Architecture

2017– AIDS memorial, Chicago
—Design proposal

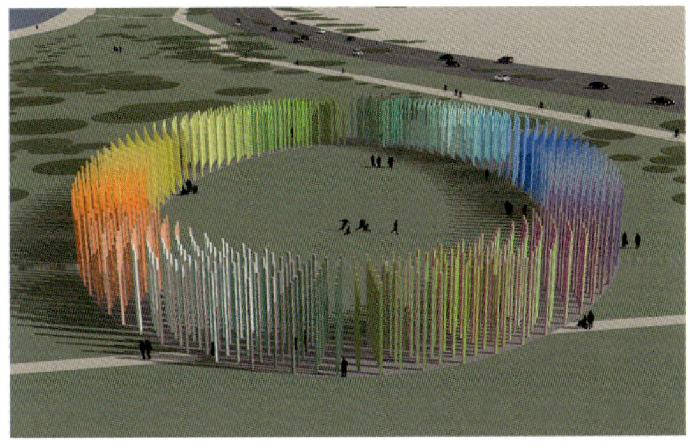

© Claude Cormier et Associés

2017–2018 Collège Ahuntsic, Montréal
—Courtyard for student center

2017–2020 The Cat Park, Toronto
—Public park for the King–Spadina neighborhood

2018–2019 Champlain Node East Park, Ottawa
—Park for a site bordering the Ottawa River

2018–2019 Buchwald Plaza, Mount Vernon, Ohio
—Public plaza with dog fountain in historic town

2018–2019 Rice Village at Rice University, Houston, Texas
—Public realm master plan for the densification and revitalization of a 26-acre shopping-mall site

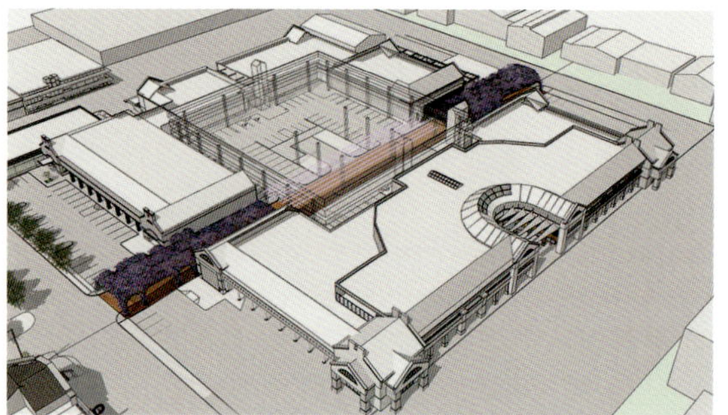

2018–2020 Main Office, National Bank of Canada, Old Montréal
—Landscape and public park design

2018–2022 2–8 Gloucester, Toronto
—Site development for residential tower in a historic district

2018–2022 Love Park, Downtown Toronto
—Winning entry in an international design competition for an urban waterfront park

2018–2022 St. Clair Block Development, Toronto
—Landscape master plan for a 3.4-acre mixed-use, three-tower development

2018–2022 West Don Lands, Toronto
—Three-tower mixed-use development on a former brownfield site

2019 National Pulse Memorial and Museum, Orlando, Florida
—Proposal for the memorial and museum to honor those killed in the 2016 nightclub attack against the LGBTQ+ community

2019 Cité archéologique, Place d'Youville, Pointe-à-Callière Museum, Montréal
—Public landscape master plan design for the museum's extension

2019–2023 1 Square Phillips, Montréal
—Landscape for luxury residential towers

2019–2027 McGill University, Montréal
—Landscape and public realm, adaptive reuse of hillside site of the former Royal Victoria Hospital on Mount Royal

Team Members

Current Team

Principal Founder

Claude Cormier

Associate Partners

Sophie Beaudoin
Marc Hallé

Administration and Communication

Liette Locas – Director
Delphine Lesage

Landscape Architects

Cloë Cousineau
Damien Dupuis
Léonard Flot
Logan Littlefield
Guillaume Paradis
Carlos Portillo
Amy René
Yannick Roberge
Yi Zhou

Past Team Members

Landscape Architects

Hélio Araujo
Margaret Baldwin
Léandre Bérubé Lebrun
Marie-Ève Cardinal
Alexander Cassini
Jasmin Corbeil
Sylvie Coutu
Lauchar Kek
Louis-Charles Lasnier
Harald Magnusson
Nicole Meier
Luu Nguyen
Georges-Étienne Parent
Mélissa Poulin
Sophie Robitaille
Marie-Claude Séguin
Valéry Simard
Guillaume Vanderveken
Annie Ypperciel

Index

Merci à Madame...
Phyllis Lambert

Claude Cormier